LESSON PLANS & TEACHER'S MANUAL
BUILDING THINKING SKILLS®
PRIMARY

SERIES TITLES
BUILDING THINKING SKILLS®—PRIMARY
BUILDING THINKING SKILLS®—BOOK 1
BUILDING THINKING SKILLS®—BOOK 2
BUILDING THINKING SKILLS®—BOOK 3 FIGURAL
BUILDING THINKING SKILLS®—BOOK 3 VERBAL

WARREN HILL & RONALD EDWARDS

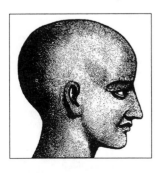

© 1987
CRITICAL THINKING BOOKS & SOFTWARE
www.criticalthinking.com
P.O. Box 448 • Pacific Grove • CA 93950-0448
Phone 800-458-4849 • FAX 831-393-3277
ISBN 0-89455-333-X
Printed in the United States of America

ABOUT THE AUTHORS

WARREN H. HILL is a Professor of Mathematics at Westfield State College in Massachusetts. Dr. Hill holds doctorates in mathematics and psychology from Peabody College for Teachers. He earned a B.Ed. at Keene State College and an M.S.T. in mathematics from the University of New Hampshire. He has been at Westfield for twenty-one years where he teaches undergraduate and graduate courses in mathematics. In addition, Dr. Hill conducts seminars for undergraduate and graduate students that focus upon the application of analytic and critical thinking to problem-solving activities and the acquisition of number, spatial, and verbal concepts by children. Prior to his college teaching, he taught for several years at the high school level. Dr. Hill presents workshops and papers at state, national, and international conferences and serves as a consultant to school districts across the country. He is the author of many articles and books on mathematics and the application of thinking skills to a wide range of academic disciplines.

RONALD R. EDWARDS is a Professor of Mathematics at Westfield State College in Massachusetts. Dr. Edwards is a Phi Beta Kappa from Brown University where he received an A.B. degree in mathematics. He also earned an M.A.T. from Wesleyan University and a Ph.D. in mathematics/education from the University of Connecticut. He has been at Westfield for twenty years teaching undergraduate courses in mathematics and computer science, conducting seminars for middle and secondary teachers, and supervising student teachers. Previous to his college teaching, he taught at the high school and junior high school levels. Dr. Edwards has conducted state and national workshops on mathematics and thinking skills and has authored numerous articles and books in mathematics/education and applications of mathematics.

TABLE OF CONTENTS

TEACHER SUGGESTIONS AND INSTRUCTIONS

Building Thinking Skills®—Primary (BTS-P), the first book in Critical Thinking Books & Software's *Building Thinking Skills®* Series, promotes the development of analytical thinking skills for children in the primary grades and introduces the skills necessary for success in the subsequent books of the *Building Thinking Skills®* Series by Sandra Parks and Howard Black.

THE COGNITIVE MODEL

Many activities in the series have their origin in the cognitive-development model delineated by Jean Piaget. A basic tenet of Piaget's cognitive model is that learning is an interactive process. Piaget maintained that the goal of education should be to provide the settings and opportunities for the learner to become actively involved in the learning process. He would conjecture, in fact, that lectures or concept demonstrations are totally useless with respect to a child's ability to understand a particular concept.

In a general sense, Piaget would maintain that learning and intellectual development are not passive, sporadic activities, but dynamic, ongoing processes. The ability to acquire knowledge is built upon the ability to organize and structure a concept's key components. Furthermore, this process is based upon the development of logical relationships. Thus, it is first necessary to identify those logical relationships that serve as the foundation of intellectual development, then to provide settings that enable the child to develop them.

Four logical relationships basic to analytical reasoning are introduced in **BTS-P** materials: similarities, sequences, classification, and analogies. Other books in *CTB&S's Analytical and Critical Thinking Skills Program* address additional aspects of intellectual development: analyzing causal relationships, making inferences, forming hypotheses, using inductive and deductive reasoning, and making generalizations based upon available information. **BTS-P** is de-signed to form a foundation for later success with these materials.

> Four logical relationships basic to analytic reasoning are introduced in **BTS-P** materials: similarities, sequences, classification, and analogies.

One keystone of Piaget's cognitive development model is the concept of *operations*. An operation can be defined as a tightly integrated system of thought processes that the child is able to apply to a concept or a situation. These operations usually begin to emerge as the child reaches six to eight years of age and are cognitive in nature, internal, and not readily observable. The task of riding a bicycle, which might be called a motor operation, can provide an appropriate analogy. If we can recall the complex motor skills and motor coordination involved in this activity, then we may begin to appreciate the complexity of a cognitive operation. By carrying the comparison one step further and recalling Piaget's position on learning as an interactive process, every person realizes that the task of learning to ride a bicycle is not accomplished by reading a manual, listening to a lecture on the skill, and observing a demonstration of riding techniques. This task is truly a "learn-by-doing" activity!

In conjunction with the concept of an operation, Piaget defines four broad periods of intellectual development. Two periods, the preoperational period (spanning the approximate age range of two to eight years) and the concrete operational period (from approximately ages six to thirteen years), are germane to **BTS-P** activities. Typically, a group of primary-grade children will include a mixture of children whose thinking is anchored within one of these two cognitive development periods. The most important revelation concerning these periods is that the thought-process differences between them are *qualitative* rather than *quantitative*. Thus, advancement from the preoperational to the concrete operational period is not simply a matter of accumulating additional facts and information; an observable change in reasoning strategies and thinking styles occurs as the student progresses from one period to the next.

A well-documented illustration of this difference is the child's ability to deal with cardinality of numbers and the associated conservation tasks. A key determinant for mastery of the conservation of number concept is the ability to recognize that the number of objects in a set is not changed by physically rearranging the objects within the set (transformations). This understanding requires an ability to compare and contrast objects (similarities and differences) and must be acquired before a child can identify changes and/or transformations between sets. A child in the pre-operational period, lacking this reasoning skill, is concerned with individual states rather than transformations and is easily misled by perceptual cues.

THE ROLE OF THE TEACHER

The *CTB&S's Analytical and Critical Thinking Skills Program* is designed to foster logical reasoning development in students. Acquisition of these skills is dependent upon the ability to verbalize and explain reasoning rather than providing a simple response. To achieve this objective, students must become active participants in the learning process.

The activities and lesson plans in **BTS-P** provide teachers an opportunity to change their role from one of reciting and/or explaining concepts to one of encouraging learners to explore and interact with concepts. This goal can be accomplished by employing those questioning techniques and discussion strategies which attempt to steer the learner in a desired direction.

To implement this philosophy, **BTS-P** activities should not be viewed as worksheet tasks for the learner to complete but rather as vehicles for generating class discussion. True thinking and reasoning abilities are acquired only by communicating and sharing ideas with others.

The role of the teacher, then, becomes one of developing questioning techniques that allow students to "wrestle" with the task of explaining their reasoning—and providing ample opportunities for them to do so. In the case of an inappropriate response, focus on the student's verbalized explanation or rationale for the answer before

> **BTS-P** activities should not be viewed as worksheet tasks for the learner to complete but rather as vehicles for generating class discussion. True thinking and reasoning abilities are acquired only by communicating and sharing ideas with others.

discussing its correctness. For example, a typical teacher reaction to an inappropriate response might be, "Why did you choose that answer?"

As a corollary to questioning techniques, the teacher must also develop acute listening skills. When an inappropriate response is given, it is often a delicate task to "hear" the student's reasoning then rechannel it toward an appropriate response. The teacher must be continually aware that there may be more than one correct response in some situations. In fact, it may be more appropriate in many cases to think in terms of a "best" response rather than a correct or incorrect response. Unanimous agreement on the "best" answer is not crucial; it *is* crucial, however, that each person understand and appreciate the other's reasoning. In sum, the role of the teacher is not to put forth a body of information but rather to serve as a catalyst between students' intuitive responses and their ability to offer a verbal rationale for their conclusions.

USING THE PROGRAM

The **BTS-P** program includes a set of Activity Sheets and a book of Lesson Plans which, when used with commercially available manipulatives, provide the teacher with daily strategies for introducing analytical reasoning into the classroom. Both the Activity Sheets and the manipulative materials are intended to be used as a vehicle for encouraging the students to begin interacting with specific reasoning skills. Development of these cognitive skills will ultimately enable the learner to apply them across the curriculum content areas.

BTS-P utilizes three sets of manipulative materials—ATTRIBUTE BLOCKS, PATTERN BLOCKS, and INTERLOCKING CUBES—to present an activity-based approach to analytical reasoning. Each lesson incorporates one set of manipulative materials in a problem-solving situation that stresses the ability to analyze figural relationships. Each activity is designed to encourage development in one of four specific analytical thinking skills: identifying similarities and differences, forming sequences and patterns, classifying groups of objects by their attributes, and creating and interpreting analogies.

BTS-P activities may be either coordinated with existing curriculum strands or used as a separate program in the elementary curriculum. If the **BTS-P** manipulatives are already used in the classroom, it will facilitate incorporating the lessons into the existing curriculum. If these manipulatives are not currently used, **BTS-P** lessons will add an important dimension to the students' growth in informal geometry and analytical thinking.

Since **BTS-P** materials are a coordinated part of the *CTB&S's Analytical and Critical Thinking Skills Program*, the activities presented in **Building Thinking Skills® Book 1** by Sandra Parks and Howard Black can be used to extend or supplement the analytical reasoning explored in **BTS-P**. Numerous activity books, written for specific manipulative materials and available from several commercial sources, may also be used to supplement **BTS-P** activities.

> Each lesson is activity oriented, incorporating the use of manipulative materials to promote analytic reasoning. The lesson's primary goal is to give the teacher and the students an opportunity to explore and share ideas.

USING THE LESSON PLANS
This teacher's manual includes a detailed Lesson Plan for each pair of Activity Sheets in **BTS-P**. Each lesson plan includes: (1) identification of the analytical thinking skill addressed; (2) student objectives for the lesson; (3) a list of manipulatives and the page numbers of corresponding **BTS-P** Activity Sheets; (4) a narrative providing the teacher with background information on the activity; and (5) a step-by-step description of a typical classroom presentation to assist students in reaching the lesson's objectives.

Each lesson is activity oriented, incorporating the use of manipulative materials to promote analytical reasoning. The lesson's primary goal is to give the teacher and the students an opportunity to explore and share ideas. Often materials, as well as ideas, are shared, for many activities require two or more students to cooperate by pooling manipulatives or ideas.

Classroom activities described in each Lesson Plan can be divided into two segments: the first portion introduces an intuitive group exploration of a particular idea using a set of manipulatives; the second portion utilizes the same manipulatives in conjunction with a pair of Activity Sheets for more formal discussion of the concept. Since the Activity Sheets follow up on the initial group explorations, it is important to explore with students the ideas presented in the Lesson Plans before they use each Activity Sheet.

The step-by-step procedures in the Lesson Plans are intended to serve merely as suggestions; teachers are encouraged to adapt the lessons to their own tastes or styles. Those teachers who have used the same manipulatives in conjunction with other activity books should find that the detailed Lesson Plans and the sequential nature of **BTS-P** provide a valuable tool for organizing these supplementary activities into a coherent program. In addition, teachers already familiar with other CTB&S materials will find that the compatibility of **BTS-P** affords them an opportunity to use these Lesson Plans as a foundation to support and reinforce their current efforts in the area of analytical reasoning.

USING THE ACTIVITY SHEETS
Although written instructions appear at the top of each Activity Sheet, they are intended to provide the teacher with a brief summary of each classroom activity described in the lesson plan and are not necessarily meant for student use. More detailed directions for the use of the Activity Sheets are presented in each accompanying Lesson Plan. If the manipulative materials described in the next section are used, drawings on the Activity Sheets are accurate. The teacher should be aware, however, that minor size variations may exist between manipulatives produced by different manufacturers.

Two Activity Sheets are provided to follow up the exploratory ideas presented in the classroom activity portion of each lesson. Teachers may wish to make overhead transparencies of some Activity Sheets to use with group presentations and to reinforce the use of manipulatives with the sheets.

Activity sheets in **BTS-P** are designed for use in conjunction with the Lesson Plans in this manual and are intended as a vehicle to generate class or group discussion, not as individual worksheets to be completed for a grade. They are not designed to be merely pencil-and-paper activities, but rather to serve as a vehicle, enabling students to use manipulatives in making the transition from concrete to pictorial format. In all cases, the teacher should stress the need to use the manipulatives in conjunction with these sheets.

USING THE MANIPULATIVE MATERIALS

Three types of manipulative materials are used in **BTS-P** to encourage analytical thinking skill development in primary-level children: PATTERN BLOCKS, ATTRIBUTE BLOCKS, and INTERLOCKING CUBES. These materials, readily available through CTB&S or distributors of educational learning materials, are already present in many primary classrooms. A conscious effort has been made to design and construct activities that maximize the use of each set and to avoid occasional use of large numbers of manipulatives that would result in excessive expenditures for materials.

PATTERN BLOCKS are manufactured in standard sizes, and a commercial set consists of 250 wooden or plastic blocks: 50 green triangles, 50 red trapezoids, 50 blue rhombuses, 50 tan rhombuses, 25 orange squares, and 25 yellow hexagons. To minimize the number of sets needed in a classroom, each Lesson Plan involving PATTERN BLOCKS is designed for a maximum of 124 blocks: 25 green triangles, 25 red trapezoids, 25 blue rhombuses, 25 tan rhombuses, 12 orange squares and 12 yellow hexagons. Each purchased collection may thus be divided to produce two equal sets of 124 blocks for student use.

The PATTERN BLOCK set contains two sets of blocks similar in shape—the blue rhombuses and the tan rhombuses. Both are referred to as rhombuses within the Lesson Plans, but since the correct color is always indicated, this should not create difficulty. At this level of development,

> [The Activity Sheets] serve as a vehicle, enabling students to use manipulatives in making the transition from concrete to pictorial format.

it is not imperative that students recognize the two rhombuses as similar shapes; while the teacher should use correct terminology, students should be allowed to identify the two blocks by color. In fact, since each of the six shapes is a different color, students will be able to complete many **BTS-P** activities using the attribute of color rather than shape. Outlines of the six shapes can be found on Activity Sheets 1–2 in **BTS-P**.

ATTRIBUTE BLOCKS are available in several different sets that differ in the sizes of the blocks, the shapes and colors used, and the number of shapes in the set. The set used in **BTS-P**, the "desktop set" manufactured by INVICTA PLASTICS LTD., may be purchased from CTB&S or from numerous educational materials distributors. The set consists of 60 molded plastic pieces and includes 5 shapes (triangle, square, rectangle, circle, and hexagon), 3 colors (red, blue, and yellow), 2 sizes (large and small), and 2 thicknesses (thick and thin).

Lesson Plans that use ATTRIBUTE BLOCKS are designed to use one set of blocks with each group of six students. The large shapes are generally used in the initial activities for each lesson, while the small shapes are most frequently used on the Activity Sheets. Outlines for the small shapes are found on Activity Sheets 3–4; outlines for the large shapes are on Activity Sheets 159–65 in **BTS-P**.

INTERLOCKING CUBES are plastic linking cubes available in a commercial set that consists of 100 cubes: 10 cubes in each of 10 colors. To minimize the number of necessary sets, the Lesson Plans require a maximum of six different colors and 20 cubes of each color. Based on this configuration, a class of 24 students would need six sets of cubes (600 cubes). These sets can then be combined and rearranged to provide each group of six students with 120 blocks—20 cubes in each of six different colors—before beginning the program.

During the separation process, attempt to place light and dark shades of the same color in sets to be used by different groups of students. The following example illustrates a sorting that would create the four sets necessary for 24 students:

- red, dark blue, dark green, orange, yellow, white
- red, dark blue, dark green, orange, black, white
- pink, light blue, light green, black, yellow, white
- pink, light blue, light green, orange, black, yellow

This sorting requires 480 cubes, thus yielding a fifth set of 120 cubes (no orange, yellow, black, or white) that can be used by the teacher.

A major benefit of INTERLOCKING CUBES is the ability to link the cubes into a variety of figures—rectangles, squares, letters of the alphabet, or irregularly shaped regions. This permits activities that use the attributes of color, shape, and pattern to define relationships between figures. Illustrations of MULTILINK CUBE figures are found on Activity Sheets 5–6 in **BTS-P**. An examination of the figures pictured on the Activity Sheets will reveal that they do not include the "knob-ends" that are on the actual cubes. Students should be instructed to disregard these protrusions when covering and tracing figures.

Thus, the use of **BTS-P** with a class of 24 students would require the following materials:

- four sets of ATTRIBUTE BLOCKS
- two sets of PATTERN BLOCKS—250 per set to be divided into four sets of 124 blocks
- six sets of INTERLOCKING CUBES—100 per set of 10 colors to be divided into four sets of 120 cubes with six colors

One additional set of each manipulative should be available for the teacher.

THE ROLE OF TERMINOLOGY

The role of language and mathematical terminology when referring to manipulative materials requires some comment. The geometric shapes in the various sets are identified as squares, rectangles, circles, triangles, hexagons, trapezoids, rhombuses, or cubes. In a precise mathematical sense, the PATTERN BLOCK referred to as a square is actually a three-dimensional solid and does not satisfy the geometric definition of a square. As a periodic reminder of this dilemma, ATTRIBUTE BLOCK Lesson Plans refer to the blocks as square shapes, circle shapes, etc. Teachers may choose to use the same terminology with PATTERN BLOCKS. At this level, however, it is not unreasonable for the teacher to identify all blocks as square, circle, etc. It is not even imperative that the students be required to use the same terminology in their discussions.

The pictured shapes on the Activity Sheets do correspond to their appropriate geometric definitions. In a technical sense, however, each block is placed *in* the interior of the shape rather than *on* the shape. The thick outlines of the shapes and figures pictured on the Activity Sheets are intended to compensate for any minor variations found in the constructions of the manipulatives. Again, although the teacher should be aware of this discrepancy, there are no compelling reasons to discuss the distinction with the students.

SUPPLEMENTARY MATERIALS

Many exercises presented in **BTS-P** include the task of tracing blocks and coloring the resulting pictures. Since most solutions give rise to figures or patterns based on shape or color, these drawings provide students a means of visually verifying the appropriateness of their responses and assist the teacher in evaluating the students' progress.

A variety of supplementary manipulative materials are commercially available for use with the Activity Sheets: rubber stamps for PATTERN BLOCKS; templates for ATTRIBUTE BLOCKS and PATTERN BLOCKS; and templates of two-centimeter squares for INTERLOCKING CUBE reproduction. These materials provide alternatives to tracing the actual blocks. Two-centimeter colored squares, to represent INTERLOCKING CUBES, and colored PATTERN BLOCK shapes can be obtained for use with an overhead projector. This array of materials, combined with teacher-made transparencies of appropriate Activity Sheets, will assist in meeting the objectives of each lesson.

BUILDING THINKING SKILLS™
LESSON PLANS—PRIMARY

SIMILARITIES

Matching Shapes (Activity 1–2)

Objectives:
> Using PATTERN BLOCKS:
> 1. sort by shape
> 2. match shapes with pictures

Materials:
> For each group of six students • One set of PATTERN BLOCKS
>
> For each student
> - Activity Sheets 1–2
> - Yellow, red, blue, green, and orange crayons
> - One container

Teacher Instructions:
> This activity is designed to introduce the students to PATTERN BLOCK shapes. The blocks should be divided among the class so each student has access to several pieces of each of the six shapes. Identifying the properties of the various PATTERN BLOCKS is an important component of this activity. This eventually leads to comparing shapes and exploring the similarities and differences between them. After discussing the properties of the blocks and placing them in the containers, work with individual students on Activity Sheet 1. Stress that the students should cover the picture of each shape on the Activity Sheet with the actual block before they color them. Students should then work independently on Activity Sheet 2.

Classroom Activity:
> Hold up a **trapezoid** (red) from a set of PATTERN BLOCKS. Ask the students to find a block in their set that is the same shape and hold it up. Verify that each student has selected the correct block and discuss its properties, e.g., color, number of sides, slanted sides. Then have the students place the block in their containers. Repeat this activity, using different shapes, until all shapes have been discussed and each student's container has two complete sets of the six shapes (twelve blocks).
>
> After distributing Activity Sheet 1 and crayons, ask the students to select a block from their containers, fit the block on its matching picture on the sheet, and color the picture the same color as the block. They should then return the block to their containers, select a differently shaped block, and repeat the process. As students work, verify their responses by checking the colors of the pictures on the sheet. Assist students who have difficulty selecting the correct blocks. Upon completion of Activity Sheet 1, allow students to continue the task using Activity Sheet 2.

Matching Shapes (Activity 3–4)

Objectives:

Using ATTRIBUTE BLOCKS:
1. sort by size, color, and shape
2. match shapes with pictures

Materials:

For each group of six students • One set of ATTRIBUTE BLOCKS

For each student   • Activity Sheets 3–4
                                    • Red, blue, and yellow crayons

Teacher Instructions:

This activity, a continuation of the previous lesson with ATTRIBUTE BLOCKS replacing PATTERN BLOCKS, is designed to introduce students to the five ATTRIBUTE BLOCK shapes. The first segment of the activity uses the large blocks, while the Activity Sheets require the small blocks. This activity encourages the students to base their block selection on shape while ignoring color and thickness.

Classroom Activity:

Separate the ATTRIBUTE BLOCKS into large and small blocks and return the small blocks to their containers. Ask each group of six students to sort the large blocks by color. Each pair of students will share ten blocks of the same color—two circles, two triangles, two squares, two rectangles, and two hexagons. Hold up a **blue triangle-shape** and ask each student to find the same shape in their set of blocks. Since some pairs of students have only red (or yellow) blocks, they must select a triangle-shape that is not blue. Discuss with the students that shape is the only attribute being matched; color and thickness are not being considered. If students select an incorrect shape, ask them to test their selection by placing their block on your block. Students who have chosen the correct shape can verify their selection in this manner. Hold up a different shape (and color), and continue this procedure until all five shapes have been used. Concentrate on the attribute of shape while stressing that color and thickness can be disregarded.

Remove the small blocks from the containers, returning the large blocks to their proper sections. Again, ask the students to sort the blocks by color to provide each pair of students with ten blocks. Students in different pairs should then exchange matching shapes until each pair has some blocks of each of the three colors. After distributing Activity Sheet 3 and crayons, ask each student to select a block from their set, find the picture of the shape on the sheet, and color it the same color as their block. Students should then select a second shape and repeat the task. Upon completion of Activity Sheet 3, allow students to work independently or in small groups on Activity Sheet 4.

Matching Shapes (Activity 5–6)

Objectives:
　　Using INTERLOCKING CUBES:
　　　　1. construct matching figures
　　　　2. match figures with pictures

Materials:
　　For each group of six students　• One set of INTERLOCKING CUBES

　　For each student　　　　　　　• Activity Sheets 5–6
　　　　　　　　　　　　　　　　　• Crayons the same colors as the cubes

Teacher Instructions:
　　This activity extends the previous lesson, with INTERLOCKING CUBES replacing ATTRIBUTE BLOCKS. It is designed to introduce students to the construction of INTERLOCKING CUBE figures. Students may need time prior to this lesson to master techniques for linking the cubes. As students construct the figures for each Activity Sheet, they should not disassemble any figures until the sheet has been completed. This permits teacher verification of responses. Since some activities require more than five cubes, judicious color selection for some constructions is necessary. Students may need to pool or exchange cubes to complete the tasks. Students should be encouraged to verbalize the properties of each figure as it is constructed, e.g., number of cubes, shape.

Classroom Activity:
　　Hold up two **blue** INTERLOCKING CUBES. With students working in pairs, ask each student to select a cube of the same color from the pile. Link the two cubes together and ask the students to do the same. Continue linking blue cubes until a length of six cubes has been constructed by each pair of stu-dents. Allow the students time to construct several lengths of six with other colors. Ask pairs of students to construct a length of two with **red** INTER-LOCKING CUBES. Select a third red cube, construct an **L**-shape by connecting the third cube to the length of two, and have students copy the figure. Connect a fourth cube to make the figure a two-by-two-cube square. Again, ask students to copy your figure. Pairs of students can then make up their own figures, exchange constructions, and reproduce each other's figures.

　　After distributing Activity Sheet 5, ask students to use two cubes of the same color to construct a figure that matches the first picture on the sheet. After they color the picture to match their cubes, ask them to choose cubes of a different color to construct the next figure. Continue to construct and color the pictures using six other colors. After completing this sheet, students should work in pairs to complete Activity Sheet 6. Verify student responses by comparing their constructions to the colors of the various pictures of figures.

Matching Shapes (Activity 7–8)

Objectives:
Using PATTERN BLOCKS:
1. match shapes
2. compare shapes
3. match shapes with pictures

Materials:
For each group of six students • One set of PATTERN BLOCKS

For each student   • Activity Sheets 7–8
                                                          • Crayons
                                                          • A container

Teacher Instructions:
This activity uses PATTERN BLOCKS to introduce the task of comparing and matching shapes. The review of PATTERN BLOCK shapes also introduces the concept that the blocks can be turned and flipped without changing shape. Explicit reference should be made to these types of motion, since Activity Sheet 8 includes the matching of shapes in different positions. Students are also asked to construct sets of three blocks to place in their individual containers. This task is intended to introduce elementary number ideas, but if students encounter difficulty, one block at a time can be held up by the teacher, and students can place the corresponding shape in their containers.

Classroom Activity:
Review the PATTERN BLOCK shapes by holding up each shape and asking students to locate a block that has the same shape. Repeat this procedure several times, turning and flipping the blocks to show different positions. Finally, hold up each shape and ask the students to select three blocks that have the same shape to place in their containers. Verify that students have placed the correct shape and number of blocks in their individual containers.

Distribute Activity Sheet 7 and ask the students to select from their container a block that has the same shape as the shaded shape in Row **A**. Have the students place the block on the shaded shape, then ask them to find another picture of the shape in the same row. Encourage students to explain why the other shapes do not match (different number of sides, etc.). After coloring the picture to match the color of the block, repeat the activity with Rows **B** and **C**. Encourage students to verbalize their reasons for selecting a particular shape. After the students complete Activity Sheet 7, have them continue the task with rows **A–D** on Activity Sheet 8. Stress to students that the blocks may be turned or flipped to a different position.

Matching Shapes (Activity 9–10)

Objectives:
> Using ATTRIBUTE BLOCKS:
> 1. sort by color, size, and thickness
> 2. discriminate between different shapes
> 3. match shapes with pictures

Materials:
> For each group of six students • One set of ATTRIBUTE BLOCKS
>
> For each student   • Activity Sheets 9–10
>   • Crayons

Teacher Instructions:
> This activity continues the previous lesson, with ATTRIBUTE BLOCKS replacing PATTERN BLOCKS. It is designed to reinforce the task of shape discrimination. Preliminary activities require that students sort the ATTRIBUTE BLOCKS by color, size, and thickness. The first segment of this lesson uses the large blocks, while the Activity Sheets require the small blocks. Continue to encourage the students to discuss their reasons for selecting a particular block, concentrating on the attributes of shape and color.

Classroom Activity:
> After separating the ATTRIBUTE BLOCKS into large and small shapes, return the small blocks to their containers. Ask each group of six students to sort the large blocks first by color, then by thickness. Each student should have five blocks of the same color and thickness. Hold up a **blue hexagon-shape** and ask the students to find the same shape in their sets of blocks. Since some students have only red (or yellow) blocks, they must select a hexagon-shape that is not blue. You may need to review the fact that shape is the only attribute being matched; color and thickness are not considered at this point. If students select an incorrect shape, ask them to test their selection by placing their block on your block. Students having the correct shape can also verify their selection in this manner. Continue this procedure until all five shapes have been used.
>
> Remove the small blocks from their containers and return the large blocks to their proper sections. Again, ask the students to sort the blocks first by color, then by thickness, to provide each student with five blocks. After distributing Activity Sheet 9 and crayons, ask the students to select a block that matches the shaded shape in Row **A**. Students should then locate a matching shape in that row by moving the block to that shape and coloring it to match the block. Repeat this activity with Rows **B** and **C**. Verify student responses by checking color patterns. Assist any students having difficulty. After students complete Activity Sheet 9, allow them to work on Activity Sheet 10 independently.

Matching Shapes (Activity 11–12)

Objectives:
> Using PATTERN BLOCKS:
> 1. match shapes
> 2. compare shapes
> 3. match shapes with pictures

Materials:
> For each group of six students • One set of PATTERN BLOCKS
>
> For each student
> - Activity Sheets 11–12
> - Crayons
> - A container

Teacher Instructions:
> This activity uses PATTERN BLOCKS to continue the task of comparing and matching shapes. Awareness that PATTERN BLOCKS can be turned and flipped without any change in shape is an important part of this lesson. Explicit reference should be made to type of motion, since both Activity Sheets include matching shapes in different positions. Students are also asked to construct sets of two and three blocks to place in their individual containers. This introduces the concept that more than one block can match a given shape and continues the development of elementary number ideas. It is important that the students continue to verbalize why shapes do not match.

Classroom Activity:
> Hold up a **hexagon** (yellow) and ask the students to find two blocks in their sets that are the same shape and place them in their containers. Hold up a **trapezoid** (red) and ask the students to select three blocks that match the shape from their sets. Repeat this procedure with the remaining shapes, asking the students to select either two or three blocks of each shape to place in their containers.
>
> Distribute Activity Sheet 11. Ask the students to find a block in their container that matches the shaded shape at the top of the sheet. Work with the students to find another picture on the sheet that matches the shaded shape. (There are three correct choices.) Students should verify their choice by moving their block to the picture they select. After they color their selection, ask the students to find another matching shape on the sheet. Have them verify and color their second picture, then continue the task by asking them to locate the third matching shape. Stress that turning or flipping the block does not change its shape. Ask students if any other pictures on the sheet match the block. Encourage them to explain why the other pictures do not match the shape of the block. After they complete the exercise, distribute Activity Sheet 12 and have the students continue locating the matching shapes.

6

Matching Shapes (Activity 13–14)

Objectives:
    Using PATTERN BLOCKS:
      1. match shapes
      2. compare shapes
      3. match shapes with pictures

Materials:
    For each group of six students • One set of PATTERN BLOCKS

    For each student   • Activity Sheets 13–14
                         • Crayons
                         • A container

Teacher Instructions:
    This activity, using PATTERN BLOCKS, continues the tasks of comparing and matching shapes. Awareness that PATTERN BLOCKS can be turned or flipped without any change in shape is an important part of this lesson. Make explicit reference to these types of motions, since both Activity Sheets include matching shapes in different positions. Students are also asked to construct sets of two and three blocks to place in their individual containers. This reminds students that more than one block can match a given shape and continues the development of elementary number ideas. Students should continue to verbalize why shapes do not match.

Classroom Activity:
    Review the PATTERN BLOCK shapes used in the last activity by holding up various blocks and asking the students to collect sets of two or three blocks of each shape and deposit them in their containers. As you hold up each block, vary its position by turning or flipping, stressing that the shape is still the same.

Distribute Activity Sheet 13 and ask the students to find a block in their containers that matches the shaded shape at the top of the sheet. Work with the students to find another picture that matches the shape on the sheet. (There are two correct choices.) Students should verify their choice by moving the blocks to the picture they selected. After coloring their selection, ask them to find another matching shape on the sheet. Stress that turning or flipping the block does not change its shape. After students verify and color the second picture, ask them if any other pictures on the sheet match the block. Encourage them to explain why the other pictures do not match the shape. After students complete Activity Sheet 13, distribute Activity Sheet 14 and continue the task of locating shapes that match the shaded shape. Continue emphasizing the geometric motions of turning and flipping.

Matching Shapes (Activity 15–16)

Objectives:
Using ATTRIBUTE BLOCKS:
1. sort by size and thickness
2. compare shapes
3. match shapes with pictures

Materials:

For each group of six students • One set of ATTRIBUTE BLOCKS

For each student • Activity Sheets 15–16
• Crayons

Teacher Instructions:
This activity extends the previous lesson on shape discrimination, with ATTRIBUTE BLOCKS replacing PATTERN BLOCKS. Preliminary activities require students to sort the ATTRIBUTE BLOCKS by size and thickness. The first segment of the lesson uses the large blocks while the Activity Sheets require the small blocks.

Classroom Activity:
After separating the ATTRIBUTE BLOCKS into large and small shapes, return the small blocks to their containers. Ask each group of six to sort the large blocks by thickness. One group of three students will use the fifteen thin blocks and the other group of three will use the fifteen thick blocks.

Hold up a **red square-shape** and ask each group of three students to find three blocks from their set with the same shape. You may need to stress that shape is the only attribute being matched; color is not being considered. If a student selects an incorrect shape, ask him/her to test the selection by placing the block on your block. Students having the correct shapes can also verify their selections this way. Continue this procedure with the remaining shapes.

Remove the small blocks from their containers and return the large blocks to their proper sections. Again, ask the students to sort the blocks by thickness to provide fifteen blocks for each group of three students. After distributing Activity Sheet 15 and crayons, ask the students to find a block in their set that matches the shaded shape at the top of the sheet. Work with the students to find another picture on the sheet that matches the shaded shape. (There are four correct choices.) Students should verify their choice by moving the block to the picture they selected. After students color their selection, ask them to find another matching shape on the sheet. Stress that turning and flipping the block does not change its shape. Continue this process until all pictures that match the block have been located and colored. Encourage students to explain why the other pictures do not match the shape. After students complete the exercise, distribute Activity Sheet 16 and have them continue comparing and matching shapes.

Matching Shapes (Activity 17–18)

Objectives:
Using INTERLOCKING CUBES:
1. construct matching figures
2. match figures with pictures

Materials:
For each group of six students • One set of INTERLOCKING CUBES

For each student   • Activity Sheets 17–18
                                              • Crayons

Teacher Instructions:
This activity extends the previous lesson, with INTERLOCKING CUBES replacing ATTRIBUTE BLOCKS, and continues the tasks of comparing and matching figures. Students should again be encouraged to verbalize why some figures do not match the shaded figures. Discussions that focus on the number of cubes used or their position in the figure are appropriate. Since some figures require more than five cubes, judicious color selection might be necessary for some constructions. Students may need to pool or exchange cubes to complete the activities.

Classroom Activity:
Ask the students to select five INTERLOCKING CUBES of the same color from their set of cubes. Begin by constructing a length of five cubes, then ask each student to construct a different figure using the same five cubes. Students should compare figures to determine which students constructed matching figures. Repeat this activity using four and six cubes as time permits.

After distributing Activity Sheet 17, ask the students to use one color from their cubes to construct a figure to match the shaded figure at the top of the sheet. Work with the students to find another picture that matches their figure. (There are three correct choices.) Students should verify their choice by moving the cubes to the picture they selected. After students color their selection, ask them to find another matching figure on the sheet. Stress that turning and/or flipping the figure does not change its shape. After students verify and color the second picture, continue until they have located all figures that match the shaded figure. Encourage students to explain why the other pictures do not match the figure. After completing the sheet, distribute Activity Sheet 18 and continue the task of locating all the figures that match the shaded figure. Continue emphasizing the geometric motions of turning and flipping. Verify student responses by comparing the color of their construction to the appropriate figures.

Shapes That Do Not Match (Activity 19–20)

Objectives:
> Using PATTERN BLOCKS:
> 1. match shapes
> 2. discriminate between different shapes
> 3. find pictures of nonmatching shapes

Materials:
> For each group of six students • One set of PATTERN BLOCKS
>
> For each student   • Activity Sheets 19–20
>   • Crayons

Teacher Instructions:
> This activity extends the task of comparing and contrasting shapes to include shapes that **do not** match. Since PATTERN BLOCK shapes can be easily distinguished by color, it is important to encourage the students to describe differences between shapes in terms of other attributes as well, e.g., number of sides, angles, size. Emphasize that flipping or turning the blocks does not result in any change in shape, i.e., nonmatching shapes are defined in terms of geometric shape, not position. Continue to encourage students to analyze differences and verbalize their reasoning.

Classroom Activity:
> Select a **square** (orange) from the set of PATTERN BLOCKS and show it to the class. Ask each student to find a block in his/her set that **does not** match the one in your hand. (Students have five correct choices.) Ask various students to explain **why** their block is different from the square. Encourage them to explain differences in terms of shape rather than color. Repeat this procedure with each of the other blocks and allow students to verbalize those attributes that distinguish one block from another. If time permits, allow individual students to hold up a block and ask other students to find a block that does not match.
>
> Distribute Activity Sheet 19 and ask the students to find a matching block to cover the shaded shape in Exercise **A** (trapezoid). Students should then locate the picture of the shape that **does not** match their block. Urge students to select the picture before moving their block to verify their choice. Reinforce the concept that flipping or turning the block does not change its shape. Ask the students to color the picture of the nonmatching shape using the correct color. Repeat this activity with the shapes in Exercise **B**, continuing to stress that the position of the block does not affect its shape. After students complete the exercises, distribute Activity Sheet 20 and allow them to work independently. Verify student responses by checking the colors of the pictures.

Shapes That Do Not Match (Activity 21–22)

Objectives:
> Using ATTRIBUTE BLOCKS:
> 1. sort by color, size, and thickness
> 2. discriminate between different shapes
> 3. find pictures of nonmatching shapes

Materials:
> For each group of six students • One set of ATTRIBUTE BLOCKS
>
> For each student   • Activity Sheets 21–22
>   • Crayons

Teacher Instructions:
> This activity continues the task of shape discrimination from the previous lesson, with ATTRIBUTE BLOCKS replacing PATTERN BLOCKS. Preliminary activities require students to sort the blocks by color, size, and thickness. The first segment of the lesson uses the large blocks, while the Activity Sheets require the small blocks. As the lesson progresses, focus particular attention on the attribute of shape, since this is the criterion for discrimination used on the Activity Sheets.

Classroom Activity:
> After separating the ATTRIBUTE BLOCKS into large and small shapes, return the small blocks to their containers. Ask each group of six students to sort the large blocks first by color, then by thickness. Each student should have five blocks of the same color and thickness. Hold up a **yellow circle-shape** and ask each student to find a shape in the set of blocks that **does not** match the circle-shape. Students should select any shape that is not a circle-shape. It does not matter if the color or thickness matches your selection. Some students may select a block that has the same shape but a different color or thickness. Initially, these can be considered appropriate responses, but students' attention should be directed toward blocks that are a different shape. Repeat this procedure with other blocks as time permits.
>
> Remove the small blocks from their containers and return the large blocks to their proper sections. Again, ask the students to sort blocks by color, then thickness, to provide each student with five blocks. Distribute Activity Sheet 21, and ask the students to select a block that matches the shaded shape in Exercise **A** (circle-shape). Work with students to locate and color the shape that **does not** match the shaded shape. Encourage students to concentrate on the attribute of shape rather than color and to explain how the shape they select is different. Repeat this activity with the shapes in Exercise **B**. Verify student responses and assist students who have difficulty. After students complete both exercises, allow them to work on Activity Sheet 22 independently.

Shapes That Do Not Match (Activity 23–24)

Objectives:
Using PATTERN BLOCKS:
1. match shapes
2. discriminate between different shapes
3. find pictures of nonmatching shapes

Materials:
For each group of six students • One set of PATTERN BLOCKS

For each student   • Activity Sheets 23–24
                                                    • Crayons

Teacher Instructions:
This activity continues the task of comparing and contrasting shapes to shapes that **do not** match. As previously noted, PATTERN BLOCK shapes can be distinguished by color; thus, it is important to encourage the students to describe differences between shapes in terms of other attributes as well, e.g., number of sides, angles, size. Continue to emphasize that flipping or turning the block does not result in any change in shape, i.e., nonmatching shapes are defined in terms of geometric shape, not position. Continue encouraging students to analyze differences and to verbalize their reasoning. The initial activity can be used to continue fundamental number development through repeated construction of sets containing a specified number of blocks.

Classroom Activity:
Review the task of selecting shapes that **do not** match by holding up a **trapezoid** (red) and asking the students to find a block in their set that **does not** match it. (There are five correct choices.) Ask various students to explain why their block is different, encouraging them to explain differences in terms of shape rather than color. With students working in pairs, ask each student to choose a set of four blocks that have the same shape. Sets should differ from student to student. Students should then find a PATTERN BLOCK that **does not** belong to the set constructed by their partner. Repeat this activity as time permits.

Distribute Activity Sheet 23 and ask the students to find a block to cover the shaded shape at the top of the sheet (hexagon). The students should then locate the picture of the shape that **does not** match their block. Urge students to select the correct picture before moving their block to verify their choice. Emphasize that flipping or turning the block does not change its shape. Ask the students to find the block that covers the picture that does not match the block on the shaded shape and color the picture of that nonmatching shape. After the students complete the sheet, distribute Activity Sheet 24 and allow them to work independently. Again, stress that the position of the blocks does not affect their shapes. Verify student responses by checking the color of the pictures of nonmatching shapes.

Shapes That Do Not Match (Activity 25–26)

Objectives:
Using ATTRIBUTE BLOCKS:
1. sort by thickness
2. discriminate between shapes
3. find pictures of nonmatching shapes

Materials:
For each group of six students　• One set of ATTRIBUTE BLOCKS

For each student　　　　　　• Activity Sheets 25–26
　　　　　　　　　　　　　　　• Crayons

Teacher Instructions:
This activity continues the task of shape discrimination from the previous lesson, with ATTRIBUTE BLOCKS replacing PATTERN BLOCKS. Preliminary activities require students to sort the blocks by thickness. The first segment of the lesson uses large blocks, while the Activity Sheets require the small blocks. As the lesson progresses, focus particular attention on the attribute of shape, since this attribute is the discrimination criterion on the Activity Sheets.

Classroom Activity:
After separating the ATTRIBUTE BLOCKS into large and small shapes, return the small blocks to their containers. Ask each group of six students to sort the large blocks by thickness. One group of three students will use the fifteen thin blocks; the other group of three will use the fifteen thick blocks. Hold up a **red square-shape** and ask the students to find a shape in their set of blocks that **does not** match the square-shape. Students may select any shape that is not a square. It does not matter if the color or thickness matches your selection. Some students may select a block that is the same shape but a different color or thickness. Initially, these can be considered appropriate responses, but their attention should be directed toward blocks that are a different shape. Repeat this procedure with other blocks as time permits.

Remove the small blocks from their containers and return the large blocks to their proper sections. Again, ask the students to sort the blocks by thickness, providing each group of three with fifteen blocks. Distribute Activity Sheet 25 and ask the students to find a block that matches the shaded shape at the top of the sheet. Work with students to locate a shape that **does not** match the rectangle-shape. Urge the students to concentrate on the attribute of shape rather than color, and stress that turning and flipping the block do not change its shape. Verify student responses by checking color patterns and assist students having difficulty. Upon completion of the sheet, allow students to work independently on Activity Sheet 26.

Shapes That Do Not Match (Activity 27–28)

Objectives:
> Using INTERLOCKING CUBES:
> 1. construct matching figures
> 2. compare and contrast figures
> 3. find pictures of nonmatching figures

Materials:
> For each group of six students • One set of INTERLOCKING CUBES
>
> For each student • Activity Sheets 27–28
> • Crayons

Teacher Instructions:
> This activity continues the task of comparing and contrasting figures from the previous lesson, with INTERLOCKING CUBES replacing ATTRIBUTE BLOCKS. Again, encourage students to verbalize reasons for selecting the nonmatching figures. Discussions focusing on the number of cubes used or their position in the figure are appropriate. If students select figures that are the same shape but a different color, their responses should be considered valid until it is established that the attribute of shape is the relevant variable. Since some figures require more than five cubes, students may need to pool or exchange cubes to complete the activities.

Classroom Activity:
> Ask the students to select six INTERLOCKING CUBES of the same color from their set of cubes and to construct a figure using those six cubes. Ask one student to hold up his/her figure and ask whether other students have figures that **do not** match. Encourage students to verbalize why their figure does not match. As the lesson continues, focus on the attribute of shape rather than color. Repeat this activity as time permits, asking other students to hold up their figures.
>
> Distribute Activity Sheet 27. Ask the students to construct a figure to match the shaded figure at the top of the sheet by using cubes of the same color. Work with students to find the picture that **does not** match the shaded figure. Stress that turning and flipping do not change the figure's shape. Encourage students to explain why the figure they select does not match the shaded figure. Students should verify their choice by moving the figure over the picture they selected. Ask the students to construct the nonmatching figure using INTERLOCKING CUBES of a different color and then color the nonmatching picture. After completing Activity Sheet 27, have students use Activity Sheet 28 to continue the task of locating the figure that does not match the shaded figure. Continue emphasizing the geometric motions of turning and flipping. Verify student responses by comparing the color of their constructions to the appropriate figures.

Shapes That Do Not Match (Activity 29–30)

Objectives:

Using INTERLOCKING CUBES:
1. construct matching figures
2. compare and contrast figures
3. find pictures of nonmatching figures

Materials:

For each group of six students • One set of INTERLOCKING CUBES

For each student   • Activity Sheets 29–30
                                                   • Crayons

Teacher Instructions:

This activity continues the previous lesson, using INTERLOCKING CUBES to construct more complex figures. Encourage students to verbalize their reasons for selecting the nonmatching figure. Focus discussions on the number of cubes used or their position in the figure. If students select figures that have the same shape but a different color, their responses should be considered valid until it is established that the attribute of shape is the relevant variable. As in earlier activities, some figures require more than five cubes, so students may need to pool or exchange cubes.

Classroom Activity:

With students in groups of six, review construction of INTERLOCKING CUBE figures. Each student should select six INTERLOCKING CUBES of the same color and construct a figure. One student should then hold up a figure and ask whether other students in the group have a figure that **does not** match. Encourage students to verbalize why their figure does not match the first student's. As the lesson continues, focus on the attribute of shape rather than color. Ask each group to determine whether it is possible for each student in the group to construct a different figure. (It is.) As time permits, repeat this activity using sets containing different numbers of cubes.

Distribute Activity Sheet 29 and ask the students to use cubes of the same color to construct a figure that matches the shaded figure at the top of the sheet. Work with students to identify the picture that **does not** match their figure. Stress that turning or flipping does not change the figure's shape. Encourage students to explain why the figure they selected does not match the shaded figure. The students can verify their choice by placing the construction on the picture they selected. Ask the students to construct the nonmatching figure using INTER-LOCKING CUBES of a different color and then color it. After completing Activity Sheet 29, have the students use Activity Sheet 30 to continue locating the figure that does not match the shaded figure. Again, emphasize the geometric motions of turning and flipping, and check the colored pictures to verify student responses.

Combining Shapes (Activity 31–32)

Objectives:
Using ATTRIBUTE BLOCKS:
1. sort by size and thickness
2. match shapes
3. combine shapes to make figures

Materials:
For each group of six students • One set of ATTRIBUTE BLOCKS

For each student   • Activity Sheets 31–32
                                                      • Crayons

Teacher Instructions:
This activity uses ATTRIBUTE BLOCKS to introduce the task of combining shapes to make new figures. The students are first asked to find two shapes that match the shapes held up by the teacher and then to combine the shapes. Students should be encouraged to combine the two shapes in various ways and to describe the resulting figures. Activity Sheets 31 and 32 require the students to select the ATTRIBUTE BLOCKS that match a picture, then to determine whether they can combine these blocks to form a given figure. Encourage the students to make predictions and verbalize their reasoning before they physically combine the blocks.

Classroom Activity:
After separating the ATTRIBUTE BLOCKS into large and small shapes, return the small blocks to their containers. Ask each group of six students to sort the large blocks by thickness. One group of three students will use the fifteen thin blocks; the other group of three will use the fifteen thick blocks. Select a **rectangle-shape** and a **triangle-shape** and ask the students to find the same shapes in their piles. (They may choose a different color.) Ask the two students to put their shapes together (side-by-side) to make a new shape. Have various students describe what they have made with the two pieces, e.g., a tree, a house, an arrow, a stake. Continue this activity using different shapes until the students master the task of combining the shapes and describing the results.

Remove the small blocks from their containers and return the large blocks to their proper sections. Again, ask the students to sort the blocks by thickness to provide each group of three students with fifteen blocks. Distribute Activity Sheet 31 and ask the students to locate the blocks in their sets that match the two shaded shapes. After the students have placed their shapes on the shaded figures, ask them to predict which figures on the sheet can be made by combining their two blocks. Allow the students to verify their answers by covering the figures with the blocks and to color the shapes that can be formed by combining those blocks. Upon completion of the sheet, have the students continue the task on Activity Sheet 32.

Combining Shapes (Activity 33–34)

Objectives:
Using INTERLOCKING CUBES:
1. construct matching figures
2. combine figures to create new figures

Materials:
For each group of six students • One set of INTERLOCKING CUBES

For each student   • Activity Sheets 33–34
                                 • Crayons

Teacher Instructions:
This activity continues the task of combining figures to form new figures, with INTERLOCKING CUBES replacing ATTRIBUTE BLOCKS. Encourage students to verbalize why some of the figures cannot be made. Focus discussions on the position of the cubes in the figure. Visual cues for this task are enhanced if students construct one figure with light-colored cubes and the other with dark-colored cubes.

Classroom Activity:
Ask the students to select four INTERLOCKING CUBES of the same color from their set of cubes. Construct a length of three and add the fourth cube to form an **L-shape**. Ask the students to duplicate your figure, then, working in pairs, determine if they can combine their figures to form a rectangle. Students can also be asked to form other figures, e.g., a bridge, the letters **U** or **T**, a bench. Repeat this activity as time permits, using four and six cubes to make other combinations.

After distributing Activity Sheet 33, ask the students to use cubes of one color to construct a figure to match one of the shaded figures at the top of the sheet and use another color to construct a figure to match the other shaded figure. Work with students to locate a figure on the sheet that can be formed by combining the two constructed figures. (There are two choices.) Students should verify their choices by placing the constructions over the pictures they select. After the students color their selection, ask them to find another figure on the sheet that can be made by combining their two figures. Stress that turning and flipping do not change a figure's shape. After verifying and coloring the picture of the second figure, encourage students to explain why the other figures cannot be formed by combining the constructed figures. (One figure is constructed differently.) After students complete the sheet, distribute Activity Sheet 34 and continue the activity. Verify student responses by comparing the color of their constructions with the appropriate figures. Again, encourage students to explain why some of the pictures cannot be covered with the figures.

Combining Shapes (Activity 35–36)

Objectives:
> Using ATTRIBUTE BLOCKS:
> 1. sort by size and thickness
> 2. match shapes
> 3. combine shapes to make figures

Materials:
> For each group of six students • One set of ATTRIBUTE BLOCKS
>
> For each student   • Activity Sheets 35–36
>   • Crayons

Teacher Instructions:
> This activity uses ATTRIBUTE BLOCKS to extend the task of combining shapes
> to make new figures. After selecting shapes and combining them to make
> figures, the students are asked to select certain blocks and determine whether
> they can combine these blocks to form a given figure. Activity Sheets 35 and 36
> differ from previous lessons in that outlines of individual blocks have been
> deleted from the pictured figures. Continue to emphasize verbalization and
> making predictions before physically combining the blocks.

Classroom Activity:
> After separating the ATTRIBUTE BLOCKS into large and small shapes, return
> the small blocks to their containers. Ask each group of six students to sort the
> large blocks by thickness. One group of three will use the fifteen thin blocks
> and the other group of three will use the fifteen thick blocks. Select a **hexagon-
> shape** and a **rectangle-shape**, and ask the students to find the same shapes in
> their piles. (They may choose a different color.) Then ask the students to put
> the two shapes together (side-by-side) to make a new shape. Have students
> describe what they made with the two pieces, e.g., a tree, a person, a space
> building. Continue this activity using different shapes until the students have
> reviewed the task of combining shapes and describing the results.
>
> Remove the small blocks from their containers and return the large blocks to
> their proper sections. Again, ask the students to sort the blocks by thickness to
> provide each group of three students with fifteen blocks. Distribute Activity
> Sheet 35 and ask the students to locate the blocks in their sets that match the
> two shaded shapes. Work with the students to determine which figures can be
> made by combining those blocks. Point out that the lines that show some of the
> sides of the shapes are missing. Allow students to verify their answers by
> covering the figures with the blocks and to color those shapes which they can
> form. When students have completed the exercise, allow them to continue the
> task on Activity Sheet 36.

Combining Shapes (Activity 37–38)

Objectives:
Using PATTERN BLOCKS:
1. match shapes
2. combine shapes to make figures

Materials:
For each group of six students   • One set of PATTERN BLOCKS

For each student   • Activity Sheets 37–38
                                 • Crayons

Teacher Instructions:
This activity continues developing skills in combining shapes, with PATTERN
BLOCKS replacing ATTRIBUTE BLOCKS. The students are asked to find
two blocks that match those held by the teacher and then to combine those
blocks. Encourage the students to combine the two shapes in various ways
and describe their resulting figures. Note that combining some shapes (side-
by-side) will produce only one figure, e.g., a square and a triangle. After
completing this task, students are to select blocks to match pictures and
determine whether they can construct a given figure using those blocks. Again,
encourage students to make predictions and verbalize their reasoning before
making physical combinations.

Classroom Activity:
Select a **hexagon** (yellow) and a **triangle** (green) and ask the students to find
the same shapes in their sets. Ask the students to put the two shapes together
(side-by-side) to make a new figure. Encourage students to describe what they
have made with their shapes, e.g., a clown with a hat, a golf ball on
a tee, a chicken's head and beak. Select a **trapezoid** (red) and a **square**
(orange) and ask the students to select the same shapes from their sets. Then
have the students combine the blocks and describe the figure they have made.

Distribute Activity Sheet 37 and have the students locate blocks in their set
that match the two shaded shapes. After they have placed their blocks on the
pictures, work with students to determine which figures on the sheet can be
made by combining their blocks. Stress that the geometric motions of flipping
and/or turning are permissible. Continue encouraging students to explain why
some of the figures cannot be formed by combining their two shapes. Allow
students to verify their answers and color those figures that can be formed by
combining the two blocks. After students complete Activity Sheet 37, allow
them to work independently or in groups to complete Activity Sheet 38.

Combining Shapes (Activity 39–40)

Objectives:
Using PATTERN BLOCKS:
1. match shapes
2. combine shapes to make figures

Materials:
For each group of six students • One set of PATTERN BLOCKS

For each student   • Activity Sheets 39–40
                                                      • Crayons

Teacher Instructions:
This activity continues the concept of combining shapes using PATTERN BLOCKS. The students are first asked to find two blocks that match those held by the teacher and then to combine them. Encourage students to combine the shapes in various ways and to describe the resulting figures. Note that combining some shapes (side-by-side) will produce only one figure, e.g., a square and a triangle. After the students complete this task, they must select the blocks that match pictures and determine whether they can construct a given figure using those blocks. Encourage students to make predictions and verbalize their reasoning before making the physical combinations.

Classroom Activity:
Select a **hexagon** (yellow) and a **trapezoid** (red) and ask the students to find the same shapes in their sets. Review combining shapes by asking students to put the two shapes together (side-by-side) to make a new figure. Ask them to describe what they have made with the two pieces, e.g., a bubble gum machine, a clown with a hat, a space building. Continue this procedure with other blocks as time permits, or allow students to work in pairs, with one student constructing a figure by combining two shapes and the other constructing a matching figure.

Distribute Activity Sheet 39 and have the students locate the two blocks in their sets that match the shaded shapes. After they have placed their blocks on the shaded shapes, work with students to determine which figures on the sheet they can make by combining the two blocks. Continue to stress that the geometric motions of flipping and/or turning are permissible, and encourage students to explain why some figures cannot be formed by combining the two shapes. Allow students to verify their answers and color those figures that can be formed by combining the blocks. After students complete Activity Sheet 39, they should work independently or in small groups on Activity Sheet 40.

Combining Shapes (Activity 41–42)

Objectives:
Using PATTERN BLOCKS:
1. match three shapes
2. combine shapes to make figures

Materials:
For each group of six students • One set of PATTERN BLOCKS

For each student   • Activity Sheets 41–42
                                • Crayons

Teacher Instructions:
This activity extends the previous lesson, in which two blocks were used, by asking the students to find, then combine, three PATTERN BLOCKS. Encourage students to combine the shapes in various ways and to compare their resulting figures for similarities. After they complete this task, the students are to select blocks to match shaded shapes and determine whether they can construct a given figure using those shapes. Encourage them to make predictions and verbalize their reasoning before making the physical combinations.

Classroom Activity:
Select a **rhombus** (blue), a **trapezoid** (red), and a **triangle** (green) and ask the students to select the same shapes from their sets. Ask the students to put the triangle and rhombus together (side-by-side) to make a new shape and to describe what they have made. (The result of this combination should be a trapezoid.) Then ask the students to add the trapezoid shape to the figure to make a hexagon. Ask them what other figures they can form with these three blocks. Select a **trapezoid** (red), a **triangle** (green), and a **square** (orange), then ask the students to select the same blocks from their sets. Have them combine these three new shapes and compare results to determine how many students made the same figure. Select a student-constructed figure and ask the other students if they can construct the same figure with their three blocks. Continue this process until students are able to rearrange their blocks to match any given figure.

Distribute Activity Sheet 41 and have the students locate the three shaded shapes in their sets. After they place their blocks on the shaded shapes, ask them to predict which figures can be made by combining the PATTERN BLOCKS. Allow students to verify their answers and color those figures that they can form by combining the three blocks. After students have completed Activity Sheet 41, have them continue the task on Activity Sheet 42.

Combining Shapes (Activity 43–44)

Objectives:
    Using PATTERN BLOCKS:
      1. match two shapes
      2. combine shapes to make figures

Materials:
    For each group of six students • One set of PATTERN BLOCKS

    For each student   • Activity Sheets 43–44
                                  • Crayons

Teacher Instructions:
    This activity is a variation of the previous lesson, which involved combining three PATTERN BLOCKS to form a figure. The students are first asked to select two particular blocks, then to combine their blocks to create new figures. Encourage students to combine the two shapes in various ways and to compare the resulting figures. Many students will have similar figures. After they complete this task, the students must then select blocks that match two shaded shapes and determine whether they can construct a given figure with those blocks. Activity Sheets for this activity **do not** provide perceptual cues for positioning the individual shapes. Encourage students to make predictions and state their reasoning before making any physical combinations.

Classroom Activity:
    Select a **trapezoid** (red) and a **triangle** (green) and ask students to find the same shapes in their sets. Then ask them to put the trapezoid and the triangle together (side-by-side) to make a new figure. Have students compare their figures to determine how many have constructed the same figure. Select a student-constructed figure and ask the other students to rearrange their blocks to make the same figure. Continue this process until all students are able to rearrange their two pattern blocks to match any given figure.

    Distribute Activity Sheet 43 and have the students locate the two shaded shapes in their sets. After they place their blocks on the shaded shapes, work with them to find a figure on the sheet that can be formed by combining the two blocks. (There are two correct choices.) Allow the students to verify their answers and color the figure; then ask them to find and color another figure that can be made with the blocks. Encourage explanations of why the other figures cannot be made by combining the two blocks. After students complete Activity Sheet 43, distribute Activity Sheet 44 and allow them to work independently or in groups to continue the task. Assist students who have difficulty and encourage them to verbalize their reasoning.

Finding Shapes (Activity 45–46)

Objectives:
> Using PATTERN BLOCKS:
> 1. match shapes
> 2. locate shapes embedded in a figure

Materials:
> For each group of six students • One set of PATTERN BLOCKS
>
> For each student   • Activity Sheets 45–46
>   • Crayons

Teacher Instructions:
> This activity uses PATTERN BLOCKS to introduce the concept of finding shapes which are embedded in a larger configuration of shapes. This skill reverses the earlier procedure of combining shapes. While the initial task is simplified by the color coding of the blocks, it is important that the students experience the task of searching for a part of the whole. This activity begins to develop the concept that certain PATTERN BLOCK shapes can be constructed from other blocks in the set. (Triangles, rhombuses, trapezoids, and hexagons share common characteristics.) Later activities will extend the interrelations among these particular shapes.

Classroom Activity:
> Ask each student to select two **trapezoids** (red), two **rhombuses** (blue), and two **triangles** (green) from their PATTERN BLOCK sets and to make a figure with those blocks. Then, hold up a triangle and ask the students to find that block within their figure and take it out. Allow time to remove the block and return it to the sets. Repeat this process with the other shapes until only one trapezoid remains in their figure. Ask the students to select another particular set of blocks and construct another figure. Again, hold up various blocks from the figure for the students to locate and remove.
>
> Distribute Activity Sheet 45 and have the students choose a block to cover the shaded shape. Ask them to find a picture of that shape in Figure **A**. Stress that turning or flipping the block is permissible. Some students may cover two triangles with the rhombus. While this response is appropriate and will be encouraged in later activities, focus their attention on looking for shapes that are not subdivided. Work with students to complete and color the figures, encouraging them to make predictions and explain their answers before moving the block to the figure. After students complete the sheet, allow them to continue the task on Activity Sheet 46. Verify their responses by checking color patterns, and assist any students who encounter difficulty.

Finding Shapes (Activity 47–48)

Objectives:
Using INTERLOCKING CUBES:
1. construct figures to match a given picture
2. locate figures embedded in a rectangle

Materials:
For each group of six students • One set of INTERLOCKING CUBES

For each student   • Activity Sheets 47–48
                                             • Crayons

Teacher Instructions:
This activity uses INTERLOCKING CUBES to extend the previous task to finding figures embedded in a rectangle. The initial activity involves first constructing a rectangle, then constructing a variety of figures that are embedded in the rectangle. The embedded figures should have no cubes that extend beyond the edges of the rectangle. As students search for figures that are a part of larger figures, emphasize that the geometric motions of turning or flipping are permissible.

Classroom Activity:
Ask each pair of students to select eight INTERLOCKING CUBES of the same color from their sets and make a **two-by-four-cube** rectangle. Then ask each member of the pair to select four cubes of a different color from their sets, construct another figure with those cubes, and determine whether the new figure will cover part of the rectangle. Work with the students to construct other figures with four cubes that will cover part of the rectangle. Pairs of students may be encouraged to construct two individual figures that can be combined to cover the entire rectangle. As time permits, allow students to construct figures with five or six cubes that can be used to cover part of the rectangle. Students may be asked to explain why pairs of figures constructed with five cubes will not fit together to make the rectangle.

Distribute Activity Sheet 47 and have the students construct the shaded figure using INTERLOCKING CUBES of the same color. Ask them to find a picture of this constructed figure in the rectangle at the bottom of the sheet. (There are three correct choices.) Stress that turning or flipping the constructed figure is permissible. Allow time to color the picture of the matching figure. Then ask the students to find, verify, and color another matching figure in the rectangle. Repeat this procedure to find the third figure. Encourage students to explain why the uncolored parts of the rectangle cannot be covered with their figure. After students complete the exercise, allow them to continue the task on Activity Sheet 48. Verify their responses by checking color patterns, and assist any students who have difficulty.

Finding Shapes (Activity 49–50)

Objectives:
Using PATTERN BLOCKS:
1. match shapes
2. locate shapes within a figure

Materials:
For each group of six students • One set of PATTERN BLOCKS

For each student   • Activity Sheets 49–50
                         • Crayons

Teacher Instructions:
This activity uses PATTERN BLOCKS to extend the task of finding shapes embedded in a more complex figure. While the task is simplified by the color-coded blocks, it is important that students experience searching for a part of the whole. This activity continues developing the idea that certain PATTERN BLOCKS can be constructed from other blocks in the set. (The triangle, rhombus, trapezoid, and hexagon shapes share common characteristics.) The interrelation among these particular shapes will be extended in later lessons. Continue to emphasize that the geometric motions of turning or flipping are permissible when searching for shapes that are part of larger figures.

Classroom Activity:
Ask each pair of students to select one **hexagon** (yellow), two **trapezoids** (red), three **rhombuses** (blue), and three **triangles** (green) from their PATTERN BLOCK set. Work with the students to determine whether a shape to match the hexagon can be constructed with the two trapezoids. Repeat this process using the trapezoid and three triangles; the three rhombuses; the trapezoid, rhombus, and triangle. If time permits, work with the students to break the trapezoid and rhombus into their respective components.

Distribute Activity Sheet 49 and have the students find blocks to cover the four shapes labeled **A**, **B**, **C**, and **D** in the first exercise. Ask them to find a picture of any of these shapes in the larger figure on the left. Stress that turning and flipping the blocks are permissible. Some may attempt to cover a portion of the trapezoid with the rhombus. Explain that the block must cover the entire outline of the shape. Allow the students to color the pictures of the correct shapes; then work with them to complete the other exercise on the sheet. Encourage them to make predictions and explain their answers before moving the block to the figure. After students complete Activity Sheet 49, allow them to continue on Activity Sheet 50. Verify their responses by checking color patterns. Assist any students who encounter difficulty.

Dividing Shapes into Equal Parts (Activity 51–52)

Objectives:
Using PATTERN BLOCKS:
1. match shapes
2. combine two shapes to make a complex figure
3. divide a shape into two equal parts

Materials:
For each group of six students • One set of PATTERN BLOCKS

For each student   • Activity Sheets 51–52
                                • Crayons

Teacher Instructions:
This activity uses PATTERN BLOCKS to introduce the concept of dividing figures into equal parts. While the initial tasks allow the teacher to demonstrate dividing figures into two, three, or six equal parts, the Activity Sheets are restricted to dividing figures into two equal parts. This activity focuses on constructing figures from two matching shapes and a preliminary discussion of the relation between the figure and the shapes used to form it. Since the colors of each PATTERN BLOCK shape are the same, dividing a figure into equal parts with these blocks will not be as apparent as it will be in later lessons.

Classroom Activity:
Have the students select one **hexagon** (yellow) and two **trapezoids** (red) from their PATTERN BLOCK sets. Then ask whether they can put the two trapezoids together to form a hexagon. Encourage students to explain the relationship between the figure they constructed and the hexagon. Appropriate observations might include that each trapezoid is equal to one-half of the hexagon or that trapezoids can be used to divide a hexagon into two equal parts. Select one **rhombus** (blue) and two **triangles** (green) and repeat the activity, emphasizing that the two triangles divide the rhombus into two equal parts. If time permits, work with the students to explore the relationship between the rhombus and the hexagon, the triangle and the trapezoid, and the triangle and the hexagon.

Distribute Activity Sheet 51 and have the students choose blocks to cover the shaded shapes in Row **A**. Ask them to try combining the two triangles to make the figure. Point out that the blocks may be turned or flipped to make the figure. Class discussion should begin to develop the idea that the triangles divide the figure into equal parts. Allow the students time to draw a line dividing the picture into equal parts and to color the picture. Work with the students to complete the other rows on the page, continuing to emphasize the division of the figures into equal parts. After students complete Activity Sheet 51, verify their answers and allow them to work individually on Activity Sheet 52.

Dividing Shapes into Equal Parts (Activity 53–54)

Objectives:
Using ATTRIBUTE BLOCKS:
  1. sort shapes by size and thickness
  2. match shapes
  3. combine two shapes to make a complex figure
  4. divide a shape into two and three equal parts

Materials:
For each group of six students • One set of ATTRIBUTE BLOCKS

For each student   • Activity Sheets 53–54
                                 • Crayons

Teacher Instructions:
This activity uses ATTRIBUTE BLOCKS to continue the task of dividing figures into equal parts. The teacher should present figures that are divided into two or three equal parts, since the Activity Sheets contain similar figure division. The focus of this activity should be on constructing a figure from two matching shapes and the relationship between that figure and the shapes used to form it. Using blocks of different colors will emphasize the division of each figure into equal parts.

Classroom Activity:
After separating the ATTRIBUTE BLOCKS into large and small shapes, return the small blocks to their containers. Ask each group of six students to sort the large blocks by thickness. One group of three students will use the fifteen thin blocks and the other group of three will use the fifteen thick blocks. Hold up a figure made by combining **two blue rectangle-shapes**, and ask each group of students to construct the figure using two different colored blocks (yellow and red). Ask the students what part of their figure is yellow and what part is red. Repeat the task using two and three other shapes. Focus class discussion on the number of equal parts contained in each figure.

Remove the small blocks from their containers and return the large blocks to their proper sections. Again, ask the students to sort the blocks by thickness to provide each group of three with fifteeen blocks. Distribute Activity Sheet 53 and ask two students from each group to place a different colored block on each shaded shape in Row **A**. Ask the third student to combine these two blocks to make the pictured figure. Allow the students time to draw a line to divide the figure into equal parts and to color the corresponding parts. Encourage students to verbalize that the color pattern shows that the figure has been divided into equal parts. Work with students to complete the other rows on the sheet, emphasizing the concept of dividing each figure into equal parts. After students complete the exercises, verify their answers and allow them to work in groups on Activity Sheet 54.

Dividing Shapes into Equal Parts (Activity 55–56)

Objectives:
Using INTERLOCKING CUBES:
1. match figures
2. combine two figures to form a more complex figure
3. divide a figure into two equal parts

Materials:

For each group of six students   • One set of INTERLOCKING CUBES

For each student   • Activity Sheets 55–56
                                 • Crayons

Teacher Instructions:
This activity introduces the use of INTERLOCKING CUBES to divide irregularly shaped figures into equal parts. Students should work in pairs to construct and combine figures. Constructing each figure with cubes of a different color makes the division of the figure into equal parts more visually apparent. Allowing students to work in pairs reinforces this concept, since each student will contribute an equal part to the combined figure. Class discussion that establishes creation of equal parts is of particular importance to this activity.

Classroom Activity:
With students working in pairs and each partner using cubes of a different color, have each choose four INTERLOCKING CUBES and construct matching figures. Students should compare figures to make sure they are the same size and same shape. Then, ask each pair to combine their individual figures to make a new figure. Ask one pair of students to hold up their combined figure. Encourage the group to verbalize that the new figure consists of two equal parts and that each color makes up one-half of this figure. Repeat this process as time permits, using other student-constructed figures.

Distribute Activity Sheet 55 and have the students continue to work in pairs. Have each student construct one shaded figure from the page, with partners using different colored sets of cubes. Ask each pair to find a figure on the page that they can make by combining their two figures. (There are three correct choices.) Encourage students to make predictions before they make any physical combinations. Focus class discussion on the fact that the figure constructed by each student is one-half of the new figure. Allow the students time to draw a line that divides the figure and to color their respective portions. Continue this procedure with the remaining figures, and discuss why one of the figures cannot be constructed by combining the two matching figures. When students complete Activity Sheet 55, allow them to work in pairs on Activity Sheet 56.

Dividing Shapes into Equal Parts (Activity 57–58)

Objectives:
Using INTERLOCKING CUBES:
1. construct matching figures
2. combine two figures to form a more complex figure
3. divide a figure into two equal parts

Materials:
For each group of six students • One set of INTERLOCKING CUBES

For each student   • Activity Sheets 57–58
                                             • Crayons

Teacher Instructions:
This activity is the second in a series using INTERLOCKING CUBE figures to divide irregularly shaped figures into equal parts. It differs from the previous activity in that both figures can be constructed from the initial figures. Students should work in pairs to construct and combine the initial figures. The equal parts of the combined figure are more visually apparent if each student in a pair uses different colored cubes. Working in pairs further reinforces this concept, since each student contributes an equal part to the figure. Class discussion continues to be of particular importance.

Classroom Activity:
With students working in pairs and each partner using cubes of a different color, have each choose five INTERLOCKING CUBES and construct matching figures. Students should compare figures to make sure they are the same size and shape. Ask each pair to combine their individual figures to make a new figure; then have one pair of students hold up their figure. Ask other pairs of students whether they have a figure that matches and, if so, to identify the equal parts by color. Ask students with nonmatching figures if they could rearrange their cubes to make a matching figure. Stress that after rearranging the two parts of the "composite" figure, their shapes must match. Repeat this process as time permits.

Distribute Activity Sheet 57. With students continuing to work in pairs and partners using different colored cubes, have each student construct one of the shaded figures on the page. Ask each pair to determine whether they can make Figure **A** with their two constructions. Encourage students to make predictions before making the physical combination. Focus class discussion on the fact that the figure constructed by each student is one-half of the new figure. Allow the students time to draw a line that divides the combined figure and to color their respective portions. Repeat this procedure with Figure **B**, and discuss that constructing this figure requires turning both shaded figures. When students complete the exercises, allow them to continue working in pairs on Activity Sheet 58.

Dividing Shapes into Equal Parts (Activity 59–60)

Objectives:
> Using INTERLOCKING CUBES:
> 1. construct matching figures
> 2. combine two figures to form a more complex figure
> 3. divide a figure into two equal parts

Materials:
> For each group of six students • One set of INTERLOCKING CUBES
>
> For each group of six students • Activity Sheets 59–60
> • Crayons

Teacher Instructions:
> This activity is the last in a series using INTERLOCKING CUBES to divide irregular figures into equal parts. As in the previous activity, each figure on the Activity Sheets can be constructed from the shaded figures. Turning or flipping the shaded figures is required to construct the composite figure, thus increasing the complexity of the task. Students should work in pairs to construct and combine the shaded figures. Constructing each initial figure with cubes of a different color causes the equal parts of the combined figure to become more visually apparent. Allowing the students to work in pairs further reinforces this concept, as each student's construction becomes half of the combined figure. Class discussion should emphasize both the division into equal parts and the geometric motions of flipping or turning.

Classroom Activity:
> Help the students review the process of constructing and combining matching figures to make more complex figures. Working in pairs, with each partner using a different color, have each student use six INTERLOCKING CUBES to construct matching figures. After comparing their figures to make sure they are the same shape, ask each pair to combine their individual figures to make a new figure. Have one pair of students hold up their figure. Then ask the other pairs whether they have a figure that matches and, if so, to identify the equal parts by color. Ask those with nonmatching figures if they could rearrange their cubes to make a figure that matches the displayed figure.
>
> Distribute Activity Sheet 59. With the students continuing to work in pairs and partners using sets of different colors, ask each student to construct one of the shaded figures on the page. Work with the students to determine whether they can make Figure **A** or Figure **B** by combining their two constructions. Focus the discussion on the concepts of turning and/or flipping the original figures and on equal parts. Allow the students time to draw a line dividing the figures and color their respective portions. When students have completed the exercises, allow them to work in pairs to complete Activity Sheet 60. Check color patterns to verify answers.

Completing the Shape (Activity 61–62)

Objectives:
Using ATTRIBUTE BLOCKS:
1. find a shape to match a partially hidden shape
2. complete a shape by tracing a block

Materials:

For each group of six students • One set of ATTRIBUTE BLOCKS

For each student   • Activity Sheets 61–62
                                      • Crayons

For the teacher   • One envelope pocket (see below)

Teacher Instructions:
This activity uses ATTRIBUTE BLOCKS to introduce the task of identifying a shape when only a portion of it is visible. This encourages students to begin focusing on specific properties that differ from shape to shape. These include straightness of sides, angle comparison, and length comparison. The initial activity requires construction of an "envelope pocket" to partially hide the blocks. These are easily constructed by sealing an envelope and cutting approximately two inches from each end to create two pockets. As the activity progresses, emphasize that students may choose blocks of a different color to match the shape that is hidden.

Classroom Activity:
After separating the ATTRIBUTE BLOCKS into large and small shapes, return the small blocks to their containers. Ask each group of six students to sort the large blocks by thickness. One group of three students will use the fifteen thin blocks; the other group of three will use the fifteen thick blocks. Insert a **large blue hexagon-shape** into the envelope pocket so only a portion of the block is visible. Hold the pocket up for the students to see, and ask if they can find a block in their set that matches the block you are hiding. Emphasize that the color does not have to match. Allow students to verify their responses by removing the block from the pocket. Repeat this procedure, selecting other shapes at random.

Remove the small blocks from the containers and return the large blocks to their proper sections. Again, ask the students to sort the blocks by thickness to provide each group of three students with fifteen blocks. Distribute Activity Sheet 61 and ask the students to find a block in their sets that matches the picture of the covered block in Figure **A**. Stress that different colors may be used and encourage students to verbalize why they selected a triangle rather than one of the other block-shapes. Have them verify their answer by placing their chosen block over the picture. Allow the students time to trace the block to complete the shape and color the picture to match. Work with the students to complete the other exercises, then allow them to continue the task on Activity Sheet 62.

Completing the Shape (Activity 63–64)

Objectives:
> Using PATTERN BLOCKS:
> 1. find a shape to match a partially hidden shape
> 2. complete a shape by tracing a block

Materials:
> For each group of six students   • One set of PATTERN BLOCKS
> • Two envelope pockets
>
> For each student   • Activity Sheets 63–64
> • Crayons for each student

Teacher Instructions:
> This activity uses PATTERN BLOCKS to extend the task of recognizing and completing an incomplete shape. The initial activity is simplified by the color-coded blocks, making it possible for students to select the matching block on the basis of color rather than shape. Consequently, explanations of choices should focus on shape attributes, not color. Activity Sheet 64 introduces the concept of more than one correct response. Either of two shapes might be correctly used in Exercises **A** and **C**, while three choices are available for Exercise **D**. Encourage students to locate all blocks that would fit the picture, then to select one shape to trace and color. Construct a sufficient number of envelope pockets to provide one for each group of three students. The construction is described in **Teacher Instructions** for activity 61–62.

Classroom Activity:
> To review locating blocks that match a partially hidden block, insert a **square** (orange) into an envelope pocket, show it to the students, and ask each group to find a block that matches. Distribute one pocket envelope to each group of three students. Have one student in the group partially hide a PATTERN BLOCK in the pocket; the other two students should then locate the matching shape. Continue as time permits, allowing students to take turns hiding the blocks.
>
> Distribute Activity Sheet 63 and work with the students to identify the partially hidden block in Exercise **A**. Encourage students to systematically eliminate certain shapes from consideration and verbalize their reasoning, rather than using random trial and error. After each student locates the correct block, allow time for them to trace the block and color the picture. Work with students as needed on the remaining exercises; then distribute Activity Sheet 64.
>
> Ask the students to locate a block in their sets that matches the partially hidden shape in Exercise **A**. Discuss with the class that more than one block will fit. Each student should pick one of the matching blocks to trace and color the picture. Allow them to continue working in small groups to complete the activity. Remind the students that there may be more than one correct response.

Completing the Shape (Activity 65-66)

Objectives:
Using INTERLOCKING CUBES:
1. construct a figure to match a picture
2. find a figure that matches a partially hidden figure
3. complete a picture by tracing a figure

Materials:

For each group of six students • One set of INTERLOCKING CUBES

For each student   • Activity Sheets 65–66
                                   • Crayons for each student

For the teacher   • One envelope pocket

Teacher Instructions:
This activity uses INTERLOCKING CUBE figures to continue the task of finding figures to match partially hidden figures. Construct **one length of three** and **one two-by-two-cube square** before beginning this activity. As the activity progresses, encourage the students to focus on the attribute of shape rather than color and to explain why the constructed figures will not fit on certain pictures. Emphasize prediction and verification of matching figures rather than solutions based upon random trial and error.

Classroom Activity:
Ask the students to construct **one length of three** and **one two-by-two-cube square** using two sets of different colored INTERLOCKING CUBES. Partially hide one of your previously constructed figures in an envelope pocket. Show it to the students and ask them which of the two figures they made matches the hidden one. Stress that the color of their figures may be different, and encourage students to explain why they selected a particular figure. Repeat the activity as time permits, alternating figures and exposing different parts of each figure.

Distribute Activity Sheet 65 and ask the students to select three different colored sets of INTERLOCKING CUBES and to construct figures that match the shaded figures pictured on the sheet. Select the first figure and work with the students to determine if it fits on one of the partially hidden figures. (There are two correct choices.) Students should select one matching picture, trace the figure to complete the picture, then color the traced figure to match their constructed figure. Repeat this process with the two remaining figures. Encourage students to verbalize the reasons for their selections. After they complete the exercises, distribute Activity Sheet 66 and allow time for the students to construct the figures and complete the page. Verify student responses by checking color patterns, and assist any students who encounter difficulty.

Copying a Figure (Activity 67–68)

Objectives:

Using ATTRIBUTE BLOCKS:
1. combine shapes to form more complex figures
2. construct a figure to match a picture of a figure

Materials:

For each group of six students • One set of ATTRIBUTE BLOCKS

For each student   • Activity Sheets 67–68
                                       • Crayons

Teacher Instructions:

This activity uses ATTRIBUTE BLOCKS to introduce constructing and copying figures. Preliminary activities require the students to sort the blocks by size and thickness. The first segment of the activity uses the large blocks, while the Activity Sheets require the small blocks. Since the blocks are sorted by thickness, each group of three students will need blocks of three different colors to construct each figure. When students copy the figure, they may copy the original color pattern or you may choose to have them ignore color by requiring only that the shape of the figures match. Since one group is using thin blocks and the other group thick ones, disregard the attribute of thickness.

Classroom Activity:

After separating the ATTRIBUTE BLOCKS into large and small shapes, return the small blocks to their containers. Ask each group of six students to sort their large blocks by thickness. One group of three students will use the fifteen thin blocks, and the other group will use the fifteen thick blocks. Ask one group of three to select **three square-shapes** from their set and construct a figure using these shapes. The other group of students should then locate the same three shapes in their set and construct a matching figure. Repeat this process, selecting other sets of three matching shapes. Alternate the processes of constructing and copying figures between the groups of students.

Remove the small blocks from their containers and return the large blocks to their proper sections. Again, ask the students to sort the blocks by thickness to provide each group of three with fifteen blocks. Distribute Activity Sheet 67 and ask the students to find three blocks in their sets that they can use to construct a figure like the first picture. Stress that different colors must be used, and allow time for students to construct and color the picture. Using the same blocks, have the students reproduce and trace the figure on the bottom of the page. Verify responses by comparing the colored pictures to their constructed figure. After they complete the sheet, distribute Activity Sheet 68 and allow the students to continue the task.

Copying a Figure (Activity 69–70)

Objectives:
Using INTERLOCKING CUBES:
1. construct a figure to match a picture
2. combine figures to form more complex figures
3. combine figures to match a picture

Materials:
For each group of six students • One set of INTERLOCKING CUBES

For each student   • Activity Sheets 69–70
                                       • Crayons

Teacher Instructions:
This activity uses INTERLOCKING CUBES to continue the task of constructing and copying figures. A major component of the task, assembling figures to form rectangular shapes, begins to develop the concept of covering a surface. When students copy the figures on the Activity Sheets, you may require that the color pattern be followed or allow them to try assembling the components in other ways to find alternative solutions. This latter method is appropriate as long as the students realize they cannot disassemble the initial figures they constructed.

Classroom Activity:
Ask the students to select three sets of four cubes from different colors. From these sets, ask them to form **one length of four** cubes with one set and **two L-shaped figures** with the other two sets. Verify all constructions and ask the students to combine their three figures to make a **three-by-four-cube rectangle**. Stress that their original constructions may be turned and/or flipped, but they may not be taken apart. After students complete this activity, ask them to take their figures apart and use the same cubes to construct four new figures: **two lengths of four** from one set and **two T-shaped figures** from the other two sets. Again, ask the students to combine their four figures to made another **three-by-four-cube rectangle**.

Distribute Activity Sheet 69 and have the students construct the four shaded figures in the top picture using four sets of different colored INTERLOCKING CUBES. Allow time for students to color the picture to match their constructions. They should then use their constructed figures to make a copy of the picture in the square at the bottom of the page. Verify student responses by comparing their colored pictures with their construction. Help students see that the figures would still fit inside the square if the two T-shaped figures were interchanged. Distribute Activity Sheet 70 and allow them to continue the task. Remind the students they may turn or flip the figures, but they may not take them apart.

Copying a Figure (Activity 71–72)

Objectives:
>   Using PATTERN BLOCKS:
>   1. combine shapes to form more complex figures
>   2. construct a figure to match a picture of a figure

Materials:
>   For each group of six students • One set of PATTERN BLOCKS
>
>   For each student   • Activity Sheets 71–72
>   • Crayons

Teacher Instructions:
>   This activity uses PATTERN BLOCKS to extend the task of constructing and copying figures. Students should work in pairs during the initial activity, taking turns constructing and copying figures using several combinations of blocks. The Activity Sheets require students to reconstruct a figure using a picture as a model. These sheets differ from earlier activities in that individual shapes within the figure at the bottom of the page are not outlined. Some students may be able to select the entire set of blocks for constructing the figure before they begin the actual construction. Encourage this approach. If some encounter difficulty copying the pictures, allow them to leave their original construction intact at the top of the each sheet while they reproduce the figures on the lower portion using another set of blocks.

Classroom Activity:
>   With students working in pairs, ask each student to select five **trapezoids** (red) and three **rhombuses** (blue) from their PATTERN BLOCK set. One student should then construct a figure with these blocks and, upon completion, the other student should copy that figure. Then reverse the process, with the second student rearranging the blocks to make a new figure and the first copying the new figure. Repeat this activity using various combinations of two shapes as time permits.
>
>   Distribute Activity Sheet 71 and ask the students to determine which shapes they will need to construct the figure pictured on the sheet. Focus discussion on how many blocks of each shape will be needed to cover the picture. Work with the students to make the desired set of blocks and cover the picture. Allow them time to remove the blocks and color the picture to match the blocks. Then ask the students to use the same blocks to reproduce the picture in the space provided at the bottom of the page. Verify student responses by comparing their colored pictures with their constructions. As students complete Activity Sheet 71, distribute Activity Sheet 72 and allow them to continue the task, beginning with choosing the appropriate kind and number of blocks.

Copying a Figure (Activity 73–74)

Objectives:
Using PATTERN BLOCKS:
1. combine shapes to form more complex figures
2. construct a figure to match a picture of a figure

Materials:
For each group of six students • One set of PATTERN BLOCKS

For each group of six students • Activity Sheets 73–74
                                                • Crayons

Teacher Instructions:
This activity completes the series on constructing and copying figures. Students should work in pairs during the initial activity, taking turns constructing and copying figures with several combinations of three different PATTERN BLOCKS. The Activity Sheets require students to use a picture as a model for reconstructing a figure. As in the previous activity, the shape outlines have been deleted from the lower portion of the page. Activity Sheet 74 incorporates three different shapes. Some students may be able to select the entire set of blocks they need before they begin actual construction. Encourage this approach. If some encounter difficulty copying a picture, allow them to leave their original construction intact at the top of each sheet and reconstruct the matching figure using another set of blocks.

Classroom Activity:
With students working in pairs, review constructing and copying figures using PATTERN BLOCKS. One student should begin by making three sets of three or four different shaped blocks. That student should construct a figure with the blocks and, upon completion, the other student should copy the figure by selecting additional blocks from the set. The process should then be reversed, with the second student rearranging the blocks to make a new figure and the first student reproducing that new figure. Repeat this activity, using various block combinations as time permits.

Distribute Activity Sheet 73. Ask the students to determine which blocks they will need to construct the figure on the sheet. Focus discussion on how many blocks of each shape will be needed to cover the picture. Work with the students to determine the desired block set and cover the picture. Allow them time to remove the blocks and color the picture to match. Then ask the students to use the same blocks to reproduce the picture in the space on the lower portion of the page. Verify their responses by comparing their colored picture with their construction. After students complete Activity Sheet 73, distribute Activity Sheet 74 and allow them to continue the task. Since this figure is large, students should reconstruct this pattern on a separate sheet of paper.

Covering a Figure (Activity 75–76)

Objectives:
Using PATTERN BLOCKS:
1. make a complex figure
2. combine shapes to fill a region

Materials:
For each group of six students   • One set of PATTERN BLOCKS

For each student   • Activity Sheets 75–76

Teacher Instructions:
This activity uses PATTERN BLOCKS to introduce the task of covering (tiling) a region with a single shape. The initial activity requires students to work in pairs to review the relationship between certain PATTERN BLOCKS. Since the tasks on the Activity Sheets require a large number of blocks, each group will need to work simultaneously on the two sheets. The additional task of covering the figures on the sheets with other shapes has been included to increase the level of activity. Activity Sheet 75 requires ten hexagons (or twenty trapezoids), while Activity Sheet 76 requires twenty triangles (or nine rhombuses).

Classroom Activity:
Work with the students to review the relationship between certain PATTERN BLOCKS (hexagons, trapezoids, rhombuses, and triangles) by constructing each larger shape from its smaller components. Then, with students working in pairs, ask one student in each pair to select **two hexagons** (yellow) from the set of blocks and construct a figure with them. The other student should then duplicate the figure using two other hexagons from the same set. Reverse the roles and have the students repeat this task, with one student constructing a figure from **four trapezoids** and the other duplicating the figure with other trapezoids. Other combinations can be made using four triangles or four rhombuses. Larger figures—consisting of up to six hexagons or twelve of any other shape—can be constructed if each pair of students within a group is assigned different shapes.

Distribute Activity Sheets 75 and 76. While one group of three students works on Activity Sheet 75, the other group of three should complete Activity Sheet 76. Ask the first group to select all the hexagons and trapezoids from their set of blocks and the second group to select all the triangles and blue rhombuses from the same set. Students in the first group should take turns covering their figure with hexagons, while members of the other group perform a similar task with triangles on their sheet. When students complete their tasks, ask the first group to try covering their figure with trapezoids, and ask the second group to identify any figures that cannot be completely covered with rhombuses (Figures **B** and **D**). Groups should then exchange their sets of blocks and repeat the tasks for the remaining Activity Sheet.

Covering a Figure (Activity 77–78)

Objectives:
Using PATTERN BLOCKS:
1. make a complex figure
2. combine shapes to fill a region

Materials:

For each group of six students • One set of PATTERN BLOCKS

For each student   • Activity Sheets 77–78

Teacher Instructions:
This activity continues the use of PATTERN BLOCKS for covering (tiling) a region with a single shape. Begin with students working in pairs to review constructing figures with different PATTERN BLOCKS. Since the tasks on the Activity Sheets require a large number of blocks, each group of students will need to work simultaneously on the two sheets. There are a sufficient number of blocks for each group of three to cover the top figure on each page, but only enough blocks for two students at a time to cover the second figure. Activity Sheet 77 requires sixteen rhombuses, while Activity Sheet 78 requires eighteen trapezoids.

Classroom Activity:
Ask one student in each pair to select **two hexagons** (yellow) from the set of PATTERN BLOCKS and construct a figure with them. The other student in each pair should then construct the same shape using **triangles** (green) from the same set. Reverse the roles and repeat the task with the second student constructing a figure with **four hexagons** and the other student reproducing the figure with **trapezoids** (red). Repeat this activity using various shapes as time permits. Other possible combinations include two hexagons reproduced with rhombuses, four rhombuses reproduced with triangles, and three trapezoids reproduced with triangles. Larger figures—using up to four hexagons and eight of any other shape—can be constructed if each pair of students in the group is assigned specific pairs of shapes.

Distribute Activity Sheets 77 and 78. As one group of three students works on Activity Sheet 77, the other group of three should complete Activity Sheet 78. Ask the first group to select all the rhombuses from their PATTERN BLOCK set while the other group selects all the trapezoids from the same set. Students in the first group should cover the top figure on sheet 77 with blue rhombuses, while the other group uses trapezoids to perform a similar task on sheet 78. Students in each group should take turns covering the second figure on each sheet, then exchange sets of blocks and repeat the tasks for their remaining Activity Sheet.

Covering a Figure (Activity 79–80)

Objectives:
Using INTERLOCKING CUBES:
1. construct figures
2. combine figures to make more complex figures
3. cover a region with figures

Materials:
For each group of six students • One set of INTERLOCKING CUBES

For each student   • Activity Sheets 79–80
                                  • Crayons

Teacher Instructions:
This activity uses INTERLOCKING CUBES to continue the task of covering (tiling) a region. A major part of this task is assembling the figures needed to cover a rectangular region. Since all initial figures on the Activity Sheets are the same shape (but different colors), student designs will vary as they cover the regions. Students may also be asked to rearrange their completed pattern to match that of another student. Emphasize that the geometric motions of turning or flipping are permissible, but students may not disassemble their original figures.

Classroom Activity:
Ask the students to make three sets of five cubes from different colors. From these sets, ask them to construct: (1) a **T-shape** using four cubes from one set, (2) an **L-shape** using five cubes from the second set (a length with four cubes and the fifth cube perpendicular), and (3) an **L-shape** using three cubes from the third set. Verify their constructions, then ask them to combine these figures to make a 3 x 4 rectangle. Stress that the individual figures may be turned and flipped to make the construction, but they may not be taken apart. After students complete the activity, ask them to take their figures apart and construct three new figures: (1) a **2 x 2 square**, (2) an **L-shape** using five cubes (described above), and (3) an **L-shape** using three cubes. Again, ask the students to combine these new figures into another 3 x 4 rectangle. Assist any students having difficulty.

Distribute Activity Sheet 79 and ask the students to use a different color of INTERLOCKING CUBES to construct each of the four shaded figures at the top of the sheet. Allow them time to color the pictures to match their constructions, then ask them to use their constructed figures to cover the rectangular region at the bottom of the page. Have the students trace the outlines of their figures within the rectangle and color the picture to match their INTERLOCKING colors. Verify student responses by comparing their colored picture with their construction. Stress that the figures may be put together many different ways and ask students to compare designs. When they complete Activity Sheet 79, distribute Activity Sheet 80 and allow them to continue the task. Remind the students that they may turn or flip the figures, but they may not take them apart.

Copying a Reduced Figure (Activity 81–82)

Objectives:
> Using ATTRIBUTE BLOCKS:
> 1. sort by size and thickness
> 2. construct figures to match pictures

Materials:
> For each group of six students • One set of ATTRIBUTE BLOCKS
>
> For each student   • Activity Sheets 81–82
>   • Crayons

Teacher Instructions:
> This activity uses ATTRIBUTE BLOCKS to reintroduce the task of reconstructing a figure from a picture. The Activity Sheets are more complex because the shapes pictured have been reduced in size and the blocks will no longer fit exactly on the pictures. This introduces the concept of figures that have the same shape but a different size. The figures pictured on Activity Sheet 82 contain incomplete shapes, further reducing perceptual cues for this task. Because of the size reduction in the pictured figures, some students should construct the figures with the small blocks while others use large blocks.

Classroom Activity:
> Sort the ATTRIBUTE BLOCK set into thin and thick shapes to provide each group of three students with a set of thirty blocks—fifteen large and fifteen small. Ask one student in each group to select three matching small shapes from the set and construct a figure. The other two students should then copy that figure using the large blocks. Encourage them to compare the figures constructed with different sized blocks and to verbalize the relationship between their respective figures. Ask another student in the group to select a set of three small blocks having different shapes and construct a new figure. Again, ask the other two students to copy the figure using the large blocks. Repeat this activity with various shapes as time permits.
>
> Separate the set of ATTRIBUTE BLOCKS first by size (large/small), then by thickness (thick/thin). One pair of students will use small thin shapes, a second pair will use large thin shapes, and the third pair will use large thick shapes. After distributing Activity Sheet 81, allow students to work in pairs to decide which ATTRIBUTE BLOCKS they will need to construct Figure **A**. Stress that the blocks in the picture are smaller than their shapes. Work with the students to reproduce the figure with their blocks and to color the picture to match their construction. Encourage the students using the large blocks to compare their figures with those constructed by the students using small blocks and with the pictures on the sheet. Continue assisting the students with other figures on the page; then distribute Activity Sheet 82 and allow them to continue working independently on the task.

Copying a Reduced Figure (Activity 83–84)

Objectives:
Using PATTERN BLOCKS:
1. construct matching figures
2. construct figures from a picture

Materials:
For each group of six students • One set of PATTERN BLOCKS

For each student   • Activity Sheets 83–84

Teacher Instructions:
This activity uses PATTERN BLOCKS to continue the task of copying pictures of figures. Since the size of the pictured shapes has been reduced and the blocks will no longer fit directly within the pictures, the Activity Sheets are more complex. This reinforces the concept of figures with the same shape but a different size. Activity Sheet 84 contains incomplete shapes, further reducing perceptual cues for this task. Activity Sheet 83 requires students to work in groups of three, since each set contains an insufficient number of blocks to allow each student to make the figures. Encourage students to identify the shapes required to copy each pictured figure and to select the correct number of blocks before they start construction.

Classroom Activity:
Review the task of constructing figures from PATTERN BLOCKS by asking each student to select **four trapezoids** (red), **three rhombuses** (blue), and **four triangles** (green) from their set of blocks. With the students working in groups of three, have one student in each group use these blocks to construct a figure for the other students in the group to copy. Next, ask a second student in each group to rearrange the blocks into a new figure for the other two students to copy. Repeat this activity as time permits, varying the block combinations.

Distribute Activity Sheet 83 and discuss with the students that the pictured shapes are smaller than their PATTERN BLOCKS. Ask each trio of students to look at Figure **A** and choose two blocks from their set that are the same shape as the blocks pictured. Encourage students to verbalize the fact that the blocks and the pictured shapes are the same shape but a different size. Before the students reproduce the figure, work with them to select the correct number of blocks for their construction. Continue working with the students on the task of selecting blocks and copying the other figures on the page. If time permits, allow them to color the pictures to match their figures. As students complete the exercises, distribute Activity Sheet 84 and allow them to continue the task.

SEQUENCES

Tracking (Activity 85–86)

Objectives:
> Using ATTRIBUTE BLOCKS:
> 1. match blocks with pictures of shapes
> 2. trace a path to connect matching shapes

Materials:
> For each group of six students • One set of ATTRIBUTE BLOCKS
>
> For each student   • Activity Sheets 85–86
>   • Crayons

Teacher Instructions:
> This lesson uses ATTRIBUTE BLOCKS to introduce preliminary sequencing tasks. The initial activity uses the large blocks, while the Activity Sheets require the small ones. Two sets of matching shapes involving three different colors are necessary for each Activity Sheet, so groups of six will need to share each block set and work in pairs to complete the sheets. Since students must build two matching rows of the same shape and color, the attribute of thickness must be ignored.

Classroom Activity:
> After separating the ATTRIBUTE BLOCKS into large and small shapes, return the small blocks to their containers. Ask each group of six to sort the large blocks by thickness. One group of three will use the fifteen thin blocks and the other group will use the fifteen thick blocks. Ask each student to select five shapes with three different colors from their sets and construct a row using their shapes while you do the same. The sequence of shapes should differ from row to row. Point to a block in your row and ask the students if they have a block with the same shape and same color in their row. Discuss the fact that some students have the same shape but a different color. Select another block in your row and repeat the process. Allow pairs of students to compare their rows and look for blocks with the same color and same shape.
>
> Distribute Activity Sheet 85, remove the small blocks from their containers, and return the large blocks to their proper locations. With the students working in pairs, ask one student to select three different colors of blocks to match the shapes at the top of their sheet. The other student in each pair should then select three blocks with the same color and same shape. Ask the first student to place his/her blocks on the pictures at the top of the sheet and the other student to cover the pictures at the bottom. Students should then color their respective rows and trace the paths connecting the matching shapes. Repeat the activity using the second student's Activity Sheet, with the students reversing their roles. After each pair of students completes their first sheets, distribute Activity Sheet 86 and allow them to continue the task.

Tracking (Activity 87–88)

Objectives:
> Using PATTERN BLOCKS:
> 1. connect matching blocks
> 2. match blocks with pictures of shapes
> 3. trace a path to connect matching shapes

Materials:
> For each group of six students • One set of PATTERN BLOCKS
>
> For each student
> - Activity Sheets 87–88
> - An 18-inch piece of string or yarn
> - Crayons

Teacher Instructions:
> This lesson continues the task of constructing rows of shapes and connecting matching shapes in different rows, with PATTERN BLOCKS replacing the ATTRIBUTE BLOCKS. The initial task uses string or yarn to connect matching blocks. To make this activity more complex, provide each pair of students with five pieces of yarn that match the PATTERN BLOCK colors and require that the matching blocks be connected with the correct color. It is possible to select more than one path for each block, but this requires using some dotted path segments more than once. Encourage the students to give each block its own path.

Classroom Activity:
> With the students working in pairs, ask each student to select one of each of the six different PATTERN BLOCKS from their set and make a row with them. The block sequence in each row should differ from student to student. Ask one student in each pair to place one end of the piece of yarn on the first block in his/her row and the second student to connect the other end of the yarn to the matching block in the other row. Continue the activity, alternating the tasks between the students until all blocks have been connected.
>
> Distribute Activity Sheet 87 and work with the students to locate blocks that match the shapes pictured at the top of the sheet. Ask each student to select another block that matches the first block in the top row, trace the path from that block to the bottom row with their finger, and place the second block on the matching shape. Repeat this activity with each block in the row, assisting any students who encounter difficulty. Allow time for the students to color the pictures and the connecting paths to match the blocks. After students complete Activity Sheet 87, allow them to work individually on Activity Sheet 88.

Tracking (Activity 89–90)

Objectives:
Using ATTRIBUTE BLOCKS:
1. match blocks with pictures of shapes
2. move a block along a path
3. trace a block
4. connect matching shapes

Materials:

For each group of six students • One set of ATTRIBUTE BLOCKS

For each student   • Activity Sheets 89–90
                                             • An 18-inch piece of string or yarn
                                             • Crayons

Teacher Instructions:
This lesson using ATTRIBUTE BLOCKS extends an earlier activity and continues the tasks of constructing rows of shapes and tracing paths between matching shapes. The Activity Sheets are more complex, requiring students to move each block along a path and trace it at the end, rather than providing matching pictures at both ends of each path. Since the Activity Sheets require three different colors of blocks, groups of three students will need to share and interchange the thick and thin blocks in the set. The rows constructed by students in each trio should differ by color. It is possible to select more than one path for each block, but this requires using some dotted path segments more than once. Encourage students to give each block its own path.

Classroom Activity:
Separate the ATTRIBUTE BLOCKS into large and small shapes, and return the small blocks to their containers. With the students working in pairs, ask one of each pair to construct a row of five thin blocks that includes the five different shapes and three colors. The other student should then construct a second row with thick blocks of the same shape and same color. Ask the first student to place one end of the yarn on the first shape in his/her row and the second student to connect the other end of the yarn to the matching block in the other row. Continue the activity with the remaining blocks, alternating tasks between students as time permits.

After distributing Activity Sheet 89, remove the small blocks from their containers and return the large blocks to their proper locations. Work with the students to place the correct block on each picture at the top of the sheet. Stress that the colors of the blocks should be different, and remind students that they can interchange thick and thin shapes until they have three different colors. Students should then move the first block in the row along its path, trace it at the end, and color the matching shapes and the path connecting them. Repeat this activity with the remaining blocks in the row. After students complete the sheet, distribute Activity Sheet 90 and continue the task.

Tracking (Activity 91–92)

Objectives:
    Using PATTERN BLOCKS:
    1. match blocks to pictures of shapes
    2. move blocks along a path
    3. trace a block
    4. trace a path to connect matching shapes

Materials:
    For each group of six students • One set of PATTERN BLOCKS

    For each student   • Activity Sheets 91–92
                                    • An 18-inch piece of string or yarn
                                    • Crayons

Teacher Instructions:
    This lesson continues the previous activity with PATTERN BLOCKS replacing
    ATTRIBUTE BLOCKS. Students will again move blocks along a path, trace the
    block at the end of the path, and color the shapes and connecting path to
    match the blocks. Although it is possible to select alternative paths from the top
    to the bottom of the sheet, this requires that certain dotted segments be used
    more than once. Encourage students to give each block its own path. If this is
    done, each student-constructed row of blocks should match. Later activities
    will introduce the concept of multiple paths.

Classroom Activity:
    With students working in pairs, review the task of constructing paths between
    matching shapes. Ask each student to choose the six different shapes from the
    set of PATTERN BLOCKS and place them in a row. Ask the first student in
    each pair to place one end of the yarn on a shape in one row and the second
    student to connect the other end of the yarn to the matching block in the other
    row. Continue the activity as time permits.

    Distribute Activity Sheet 91 and work with the students in placing matching
    blocks on the shapes at the top of the sheet. Students should then move each
    block in the row, beginning with the first, along a path to the bottom of the sheet.
    Discuss the final order of the blocks in the bottom row with the students. If some
    students used different paths resulting in a different order, stress that each block
    should have its own path and that each segment of the dotted paths should be
    used only once. Have the students reverse the process, moving the blocks back
    along each path to the top of the sheet. Students should then move the first
    block along a path, trace the block at the end of its path, and color the pictures
    and connecting path to match the block. Repeat the activity with the remaining
    blocks in the row. If any students color a path segment with two different colors,
    ask them if they can choose another path for one block so that each has its own
    path. After the students complete the task, distribute Activity Sheet 92 and allow
    them to continue work independently.

Paths (Activity 93–94)

Objectives:
  Using PATTERN BLOCKS:
   1. match blocks to pictures of shapes
   2. move blocks onto corresponding shapes
   3. draw a path connecting matching blocks

Materials:
  For each group of six students • One set of PATTERN BLOCKS

  For each student   • Activity Sheets 93–94
            • An 18-inch piece of string or yarn
            • Crayons

Teacher Instructions:
  This lesson extends the previous activity by requiring students to draw a path between matching PATTERN BLOCK shapes. The initial activity asks individual students to construct an arbitrary set of three blocks and determine whether the sets constructed by two other students contain matching blocks. Students should select their blocks independently to insure that the each of the three sets contains some different shapes. The complexity of the Activity Sheets has been increased by deleting the paths (dotted lines) present in earlier activities. The geometric motions of flipping and/or turning have been reintroduced for this activity, and students should realize that these motions are permissible.

Classroom Activity:
  With students working in groups of three, review the task of constructing paths between matching shapes. Ask each student to select three different shapes from their set of PATTERN BLOCKS and place them in rows. Ask one student in the group to place one end of the yarn on a block in his/her row, then ask the others in the group whether they have a matching block. If either has a block that matches, ask that student to connect the other end of the yarn to it. Continue the activity, with one student placing one yarn end on a block and the other students looking for a matching block, until each group locates all the pairs among their rows.

  Distribute Activity Sheet 93 and work with the students to cover each shape on the sheet with a PATTERN BLOCK. Students should then move the first block in the top row to its matching shape in the bottom row, placing one block on the other. Emphasize that some blocks may have to be turned to match those in the bottom row. After all the blocks have been moved to the bottom row, have the students reverse the process, returning one set of blocks to the top row. Each student should use the appropriate crayon color to draw a path between the matching blocks in the top and bottom rows and to color the pictures. After students complete the sheet, distribute Activity Sheet 94 and allow them to work independently on the tasks.

Paths (Activity 95–96)

Objectives:
Using PATTERN BLOCKS:
1. match blocks to pictures of shapes
2. find a path between matching shapes
3. draw a path connecting matching shapes

Materials:
For each group of six students • One set of PATTERN BLOCKS

For each student   • Activity Sheets 95–96
                                 • Crayons

Teacher Instructions:
This lesson continues the activity of following paths by combining the tasks of tracking and selecting a path between matching shapes. The initial activity requires students to construct a pattern or configuration of PATTERN BLOCKS. Placing the set of blocks on a piece of construction paper or similar material might aid in limiting the size of the pattern, but the blocks should not be joined or connected for this activity. The task is similar to movements made in checkers or other simple board games. Since more than one path can be used to connect the matching shapes, the Activity Sheets have increased in complexity. Projecting a transparency of the Activity Sheets will enhance the concept explanation and development of this task.

Classroom Activity:
Working with groups of six, ask each student to choose a **hexagon** (yellow) from the set of PATTERN BLOCKS. Ask five of the students to make a pattern with their blocks, but the blocks should not be touching each other. Ask the sixth student in the group to move his/her hexagon from block to block, placing it on top of each hexagon in the pattern so that each block is covered one time. Continue the activity with blocks of other shapes, alternating the tasks among the students.

Distribute Activity Sheet 95. Work with the students to select a PATTERN BLOCK to place on the top shaded shape and to move from shape to shape along a path to reach the bottom shaded shape. Discuss with the students that several different paths (or sequences of shapes) could be used to reach the bottom shape. Students should then work individually to select a path by moving the block from picture to picture and coloring the selected shapes and path. After they complete the task, ask the students to compare their completed Activity Sheets to determine whether their paths are the same or different. Distribute Activity Sheet 96 and continue working with the students to select the correct block and locate an appropriate path. Again have students compare paths to determine whether they are the same or different.

Paths (Activity 97–98)

Objectives:
Using PATTERN BLOCKS:
1. match blocks with pictures of shapes
2. find a path between two matching shapes
3. connect matching shapes with more than one path

Materials:
For each group of six students • One set of PATTERN BLOCKS

For each student   • Activity Sheets 97–98
                                    • Crayons

Teacher Instructions:
This lesson extends the activities of tracking and following paths to the task of selecting more than one path between matching shapes. The initial activity requires students to construct a pattern or configuration using two different PATTERN BLOCKS. Placing the set of blocks on a piece of construction paper or similar material might aid in limiting the size of the pattern, but the blocks should not be joined or connected for this activity. The task of moving from block to block has been made more difficult by adding nonmatching blocks to the configuration. Since some intermediate shapes on the figure have been removed, the Activity Sheets have also increased in complexity. Projecting a transparency of the Activity Sheets will enhance the concept explanation and development of this task.

Classroom Activity:
With the students working in groups of six, ask each student to take a **trapezoid** (red) and one other block from the set of PATTERN BLOCKS. Ask five of the students to make a pattern with their blocks, but remind them that the blocks should not be touching each other. Ask the sixth student in the group to move his/her trapezoid from block to block, placing it on top of each trapezoid in the pattern so that each is covered one time. The other shapes should not be covered. Continue the activity with other combinations of blocks, alternating the tasks among the students.

Distribute Activity Sheet 97 and work with the students to choose a PATTERN BLOCK that matches the top shaded shape in Exercise **A** and to move the block through the figure to reach the bottom shaded shape. Discuss with the students that several different paths could be used to reach the bottom shape. Have the students work individually to select a path, move the block through the figure, then color that path and the shaded shapes. The students should then place their block at the top of Exercise **B**, select a different path to move the block through the figure to the bottom shape, and again color the shapes and selected path. When students complete the sheet, distribute Activity Sheet 98 and work with them to locate different paths in the two exercises.

Copying a Pattern (Activity 99–100)

Objectives:
Using INTERLOCKING CUBES:
1. construct a matching pattern
2. construct a pattern to match a picture

Materials:
For each group of six students • One set of INTERLOCKING CUBES

For each student   • Activity Sheets 99–100
                                    • Crayons

Teacher Instructions:
This lesson uses INTERLOCKING CUBES to introduce the concept of constructing a connected pattern. Encourage the students to describe the patterns in terms of alternating colors, e.g., an RBRB... pattern of cubes. The Activity Sheets require the students to transform a picture into a physical pattern by associating shaded regions with colors. It is important that the students describe each pattern in terms of how many cubes of each color are used and select the correct number of cubes before constructing each figure.

Classroom Activity:
Allow the students to work in pairs. Hold up a **red** INTERLOCKING CUBE and ask one student in each pair to select five red cubes from their set. Hold up a **blue** INTERLOCKING CUBE and ask the other student in each pair to select five blue cubes. Connect a red cube and a blue cube, then ask each pair to select matching cubes from their respective sets and link them together. Now connect a red cube to the opposite end of the blue cube, asking students with red cubes to do the same. Repeat the process, making an alternating color pattern ten cubes long. Construct some of the other patterns suggested below. If time permits, ask each student in the pair to make a pattern, then to exchange their patterns and duplicate the pattern made by their partner.

YGGYGGYGG   GGBBGGBB   OGGGOGGG   RRRBBRRRBB
BRGBRGBRG   BOOWBOOW   YYRRBBWW   PYWWPYWW

Distribute Activity Sheet 99 and divide the cubes so that each student has ten cubes, five each of two different colors. Ask each student to place a different colored cube on each shaded shape at the top of the sheet. Help the students determine how many cubes of each color will be needed to construct pattern **A**; then work with them to construct the pattern, using the two colors they selected. Allow time for coloring, then continue the activity by asking the students to disassemble the first pattern, select the appropriate number of cubes for pattern **B**, and construct it. Encourage the students to verbalize the pattern and make a set of the necessary cubes before beginning each construction. When students complete the sheet, distribute Activity Sheet 100 and continue the task.

Copying a Pattern (Activity 101–102)

Objectives:
> Using PATTERN BLOCKS:
> 1. construct a matching pattern
> 2. construct a pattern to match a picture

Materials:
> For each group of six students • One set of PATTERN BLOCKS
>
> For each student
> - Activity Sheets 101–102
> - Crayons

Teacher Instructions:
> This activity continues the tasks of constructing and copying patterns with PATTERN BLOCKS replacing INTERLOCKING CUBES. The change from cubes to blocks results in a row of separate shapes instead of a connected set. Help students focus on analyzing the patterns by shape, number of blocks used, and color pattern. Students must work on the Activity Sheets in groups of three, since six squares and eight triangles are required for the exercises on each sheet. If two sets of blocks are available for each group of six, students may work in pairs to complete the exercises. One student should cover the pictures and the other student should copy the pattern into the box. If templates are available, some students may be able to copy the patterns into the boxes using the templates rather than tracing the actual blocks.

Classroom Activity:
> Ask each student in the group to select two **hexagons** (yellow) and three **trapezoids** (red) from the set of PATTERN BLOCKS. With the students working in pairs, ask one student to place his/her blocks in a row to make a pattern, and the second student to construct a matching row. When they have finished, reverse the roles, asking the second student to rearrange his/her blocks into a different pattern and the first student to copy the new pattern. Repeat the activity using other combinations of two blocks and varying the number of pieces in each row.
>
> Distribute Activity Sheet 101 and allow the students to work in groups of three. Help them determine which blocks and how many of each shape are required to construct Row **A**. Encourage the students to define the pattern using both shape and number. Ask one student to cover the pictures with his/her blocks and the second student to copy the pattern by placing duplicate blocks in the box. While the first students trace the blocks and color the pictures, have the others use another sheet to repeat the task on Row **B**. Continue to rotate the tasks of constructing, copying, and tracing shapes until each student's Activity Sheet has been completed. Distribute Activity Sheet 102 and allow the groups to continue the tasks.

Copying a Pattern (Activity 103–104)

Objectives:
    Using ATTRIBUTE BLOCKS:
        1. construct a matching pattern
        2. construct a pattern to match a picture

Materials:
    For each group of six students • One set of ATTRIBUTE BLOCKS

    For each student   • Activity Sheets 103–104
                                                      • Crayons

Teacher Instructions:
    This activity continues the tasks of constructing and copying patterns, with ATTRIBUTE BLOCKS replacing PATTERN BLOCKS. Continue to develop the skills of analyzing patterns by the number of blocks and colors used. The initial activity requires students to use the large blocks to reproduce a pattern made with the small blocks. This task develops the ability to use blocks to copy a pictured pattern when the pictures are smaller than the actual blocks. Since each exercise on the Activity Sheets requires four matching shapes, students will need to work on different exercises and share or exchange blocks to complete the tasks.

Classroom Activity:
    Divide each group of six into pairs. Ask one student in the first pair to remove the **large triangle-shapes** and the other student to remove the **small triangle-shapes** from the set of ATTRIBUTE BLOCKS. The second pair should remove the **large** and **small hexagon-shapes,** and the third pair the **large** and **small circle-shapes**. Ask each student with the small shapes to make a pattern by placing his/her shapes in a row. The opposite student in each pair should then copy the pattern using the large blocks. Discuss with the students that the color pattern should match, even though the sizes of the blocks in the two rows differ. Ask the pairs to exchange sets of blocks and repeat the activity as time permits.

    Distribute Activity Sheets 103 and 104. Ask the students to return the large blocks to their proper locations and to remove the remaining small blocks. Discuss the attributes of the pattern in Row **A** on Activity Sheet 103 with the students (same shapes, but different colors). Continue the process with the remaining rows on the two sheets, encouraging students to verbalize which shapes and how many of each color are needed to construct the pattern. Each group should then construct and color the patterns on the two sheets. Students will need to pool and exchange blocks to complete the two sheets.

Copying a Pattern (Activity 105–106)

Objectives:

    Using PATTERN BLOCKS:
1. construct a matching pattern
2. construct a pattern to match a picture

Materials:

    For each group of six students • One set of PATTERN BLOCKS

    For each student   • Activity Sheets 105–106
                                • Crayons

Teacher Instructions:

    This activity continues the tasks of an earlier lesson and involves constructing and copying patterns with PATTERN BLOCKS. The Activity Sheets have become more difficult, since they picture shapes that are smaller than the actual blocks. Continued emphasis should be given to developing the skills of pattern analysis by shape, number of blocks, and color. Since four squares are required to complete Row **A** of Activity Sheet 105, students should work in pairs. If two sets of blocks are available for each group of six, however, students may work individually. If templates are available, some students may be able to create the patterns on the sheets by using the templates instead of tracing the actual blocks.

Classroom Activity:

    Review the task of constructing a pattern to match a row of blocks. Ask each student to select two **squares** (orange), three **triangles** (green), and three **rhombuses** (blue) from the set of PATTERN BLOCKS. With the students working in pairs, the first student should place his/her blocks in a row to make a pattern, then the second student should construct a matching row. When they have completed this task, reverse the roles, asking the second student to rearrange the blocks into a new pattern, and the first student to copy it. Repeat the activity using other combinations of three blocks and varying the number of pieces in each row.

    Distribute Activity Sheet 105 and allow the students to work in pairs. Help them determine which PATTERN BLOCKS and how many of each shape are needed to construct Row **A**. Encourage students to identify the pattern using both shape and number. One student in each pair should then select the appropriate number of squares and the other student select triangles from the set of blocks, and use the blocks to copy the pattern. Repeat the process for Row **B**, then distribute Activity Sheet 106. Allow students to work independently, exchanging sets of blocks to complete the sheet.

What Comes Next? (Activity 107–108)

Objectives:
>Using INTERLOCKING CUBES:
>1. construct a figure to match a pictured pattern
>2. add cubes to a figure to continue a pattern

Materials:
>For each group of six students • One set of INTERLOCKING CUBES
>
>For each student   • Activity Sheets 107–108
>   • Crayons

Teacher Instructions:
>This lesson reviews the task of constructing a connected pattern using INTERLOCKING CUBES, then introduces the concept of continuing a pattern by adding cubes. Prior to using the Activity Sheets, the students should become proficient at constructing lengths to form a variety of color patterns. The Activity Sheets require two different color INTERLOCKING CUBES. Stress to the students that the colors of the two sets of cubes being used by pairs may vary from group to group. Activity Sheet 108 introduces the concept of lengths placed in a vertical position. The students should be encouraged to build "towers" rather than turning the sheet sideways.

Classroom Activity:
>With the students working in pairs, ask each pair to make two sets of six INTERLOCKING CUBES, with each set a different color. The students should construct three lengths of two cubes using one of each color, then connect the lengths to form an alternating color pattern (OXOXOX). Discuss the color pattern with the students (every other cube in their length is the same color, cubes next to each other are different colors, etc.). Ask each student to disassemble their constructions, then to construct two lengths of two cubes using the same color. The pairs should then join their lengths to make an alternating pattern of two (OOXXOOXX). Encourage students to describe the color pattern, then add the remaining cubes to continue the pattern. Repeat the process using other combinations as time permits.
>
>Distribute Activity Sheet 107 and ask each student to make two sets of five cubes, each of a different color. Ask each student to place a cube of each color on the shaded shapes. Work with the students to select the six cubes needed to construct the length in Row **A.** After students have constructed the figure, ask them what cubes they need to continue the pattern, and have them add it. Then they should color the picture to match the color pattern and disassemble the length. Repeat the activity for Row **B** and encourage students to explain the color pattern formed by the cubes. The students can then work individually on the remaining exercises on the sheet. After they have finished, allow the students to continue on Activity Sheet 108.

What Comes Next? (Activity 109–110)

Objectives:
Using ATTRIBUTE BLOCKS:
1. construct a pattern to match a picture
2. add a shape to continue a pattern

Materials:
For each group of six students • One set of ATTRIBUTE BLOCKS

For each student   • Activity Sheets 109–110

Teacher Instructions:
This activity uses ATTRIBUTE BLOCKS for further instruction in constructing and extending patterns. Both the initial tasks and the Activity Sheets require the students to construct a pattern based upon shape rather than size or color. The attribute of thickness should be ignored, since both thick and thin blocks are necessary to complete several patterns. Encourage the students to describe the patterns in terms of shape and position. Stress that replacing a block in a pattern with a block that has the same shape but a different color does not affect the pattern. The geometric motions of flipping and/or turning are used on Activity Sheet 110 to introduce a different way of defining a pattern.

Classroom Activity:
Remove the ATTRIBUTE BLOCKS from the container and sort them into two sets, large and small. With the students working in pairs, ask one pair to remove the six **square-shapes** and six **circle-shapes** from the set of large blocks. Ask a second pair to remove the six **hexagon-shapes** and six **triangle-shapes** from the same set. A third pair should select the six **hexagon-shapes** and six **triangle-shapes** from the set of small blocks. Ask each student in a pair to select one set of shapes, then have the pairs place their blocks in a row to form an alternating pattern (OXOXOX…). Encourage the students to explain and describe their constructions. Repeat the activity using other combinations of two shapes.

Return all the large blocks to their proper locations, place all the small blocks in a single set, and distribute Activity Sheets 109 and 110. Help the students decide which blocks they will need to construct the pattern in Row **A** on Activity Sheet 109. With the students working in groups of three, ask two students in each trio to each select one of the two sets of blocks and construct the pattern on the third student's sheet. After they complete the pattern, the third student should choose the block that continues the pattern, place it in the dotted box, and trace it. Rotate the tasks among the three students until all rows on the two sheets are completed.

What Comes Next? (Activity 111–112)

Objectives:
> Using PATTERN BLOCKS:
> 1. construct an alternating pattern
> 2. add a shape to continue a pattern

Materials:
> For each group of six students • One set of PATTERN BLOCKS
>
> For each student   • Activity Sheets 111–112
>   • Crayons

Teacher Instructions:
> This activity continues the tasks of constructing a pattern and extending it by adding a shape at the end. The initial activity uses PATTERN BLOCKS to review the concept of alternating patterns (OXOXOX...). The concept of position as well as shape is introduced into the Activity Sheets. Constructing and extending some patterns on Activity Sheet 112 require selecting a different shape, as well as placing that shape in a different position. Remind the students that turning and/or flipping a shape is permissible, and check their progress on the last exercise on the sheet.

Classroom Activity:
> Begin with a review of the task of constructing a pattern. With the students working in pairs, ask each student to remove two **rhombuses** (blue) and three **trapezoids** (red) from the set of PATTERN BLOCKS. One student should use his/her blocks to construct an alternating pattern, and the other student should continue the pattern by adding the correct blocks to the end of the row. Repeat the process using other combinations of two blocks and rotating tasks between the students.
>
> After distributing Activity Sheet 111, discuss the pattern of blocks in Row **A** with the students, focusing on the different shapes and number of blocks needed to construct the pattern. Then ask each pair to select three **squares** (orange) and three **triangles** (green) from the set of PATTERN BLOCKS. The first student in each pair should construct Row **A** on his/her sheet by covering the pictures with the appropriate blocks. The second student should place the correct block in the dotted box, then trace it to continue the pattern. Have the students reverse roles and repeat the tasks using the second student's sheet. Both students should then color their respective rows. Continue this procedure until all rows have been completed. Distribute Activity Sheet 112 and permit students to work individually on the exercises. Remind the students that some patterns may involve both different shapes and different positions and that they may need to share blocks to complete the activity.

What Comes Next? (Activity 113–114)

Objectives:
 Using ATTRIBUTE BLOCKS:
 1. construct a pattern to match a picture
 2. add a block to continue a pattern

Materials:
 For each group of six students • One set of ATTRIBUTE BLOCKS

 For each student   • Activity Sheets 113–114
                                              • Large sheet of paper

Teacher Instructions:
 This activity uses ATTRIBUTE BLOCKS, continuing the tasks of constructing and extending patterns. The initial activity requires students to use large ATTRIBUTE BLOCKS to copy a pattern made with small blocks. This task further develops the ability to use blocks to copy a picture when the pictures are smaller than the actual blocks. Since each exercise on the Activity Sheets requires three large and three small matching shapes, students will need to work on different exercises and exchange blocks to complete the tasks.

Classroom Activity:
 Review the task of constructing a pattern from large and small ATTRIBUTE BLOCKS. Divide each group of six into pairs. Ask one student in the first pair to remove the **large rectangle-shapes** and the other student the **small rectangle-shapes** from the set of blocks. The second pair should select the **large** and **small hexagon-shapes**, and the third pair the **square-shapes**. Ask each student with the small shapes to place his/her six blocks in a row to make a pattern. The second student should then copy the pattern using the large blocks. Discuss with the students that the color pattern should match even though the size of the blocks in the two rows differs. Ask the pairs to exchange their sets of blocks and make a different pattern with the new blocks. Repeat as time permits.

 Distribute Activity Sheet 113 and ask the students to take all **large** and **small square-shapes** from the set of ATTRIBUTE BLOCKS. Discuss the attributes of the pattern in Row **A** with the students (same shapes, but different sizes). The students should then divide the set of square-shapes into two sets, each containing three large and three small shapes each. With the students working in groups of three, ask them to construct a pattern matching the picture in Row **A**, then add a block that continues the pattern. Continue the process with the remaining rows and encourage students to verbalize how many shapes of each size are needed to construct and extend each pattern. Distribute Activity Sheet 114 and allow the students to proceed, pooling and exchanging blocks to complete the sheet.

57

What Comes Next? (Activity 115–116)

Objectives:

Using INTERLOCKING CUBES:
1. construct figures and make a pattern
2. add a figure to continue a pattern

Materials:

For each group of six students • One set of INTERLOCKING CUBES

For each student   • Activity Sheets 115–116
                                                    • Crayons

Teacher Instructions:

This lesson returns to the task of constructing patterns of connected figures and continues the activity of adding figures to the end of a pattern. Encourage the students to analyze and describe the patterns in terms of color and the number of cubes in each figure. Continue to emphasize selecting the appropriate number and color of cubes needed to construct a pattern, and make the required lengths before actually creating the figure.

Classroom Activity:

Ask each student to select six cubes of the same color from the set of INTERLOCKING CUBES. With the students working in pairs, have them review constructing alternating patterns and adding cubes to continue the patterns. Ask each pair to construct a row of cubes by taking turns placing their cubes in the row to create an alternating pattern (XOXOX...). Have one student in each pair construct lengths of two with the set of cubes, then construct another alternating pattern using lengths of two separated by single cubes (XX0XX0...). Continue the task, asking the other student in each pair to also construct lengths of two, then construct an alternating pattern with the different color lengths (XXOOXX...).

Distribute Activity Sheet 115 and have the students select ten each of two different colors of INTERLOCKING CUBES. Each student should place a different colored cubes on each shaded shape at the top of the sheet. Work with the students to identify the pattern in Row **A** (single cubes, alternating colors), and encourage them to select the correct number and color of cubes before covering the pictures. Students should continue the pattern by placing the correct cube in the dotted box. Proceed to Row **B**. Encourage students to again identify the pattern (same color, different number of cubes). Each student should construct the two lengths needed for the pattern, then cover the pictures. After determining what figure continues the pattern, the figure should be constructed, placed in the dotted box, traced, and colored. When the students finish the activity, distribute Activity Sheet 116 and allow them to continue the task.

What Comes Next? (Activity 117–118)

Objectives:
Using INTERLOCKING CUBES:
1. construct figures and make a pattern
2. construct a figure to continue a pattern

Materials:
For each group of six students • One set of INTERLOCKING CUBES

For each student   • Activity Sheets 117–118
                                 • Crayons

Teacher Instructions:
This lesson continues the task of constructing patterns with connected figures and expands it to include "two-dimensional" figures. Encourage the students to analyze the patterns, describing them in terms of color and the number and locations of cubes in each figure. Continue to emphasize that the students should choose the necessary cubes to make each pattern before beginning to actually create the figure. Some patterns on the Activity Sheets can be described in terms of the geometric motions of turning and/or flipping when moving from figure to figure.

Classroom Activity:
Divide each group of six into two groups of three. Ask each student in one small group to select two **blue cubes** and one **red cube**, and connect the blue cubes to the red cube, making an L-shape. (The two cubes of the same color should not touch.) Ask each student in the second group to select two **red cubes** and one **blue cube** and join them also into an L-shape. Ask the students in each group to check their constructions to determine whether they match. Request the two groups make an alternating pattern with their figures. Have the students reassemble their L-shaped figures so that the cubes of the same color are together, then repeat the process of creating an alternating pattern.

Distribute Activity Sheet 117 and ask the students to select two sets of ten INTERLOCKING CUBES, with each set a different color. Each student should place a different color cube on each shaded shape at the top of the sheet. Work with the students to identify the pattern in Row **A**. (The colors alternate in each figure.) Encourage students to select the correct numbers and colors of cubes needed for the first figure, then construct that figure. Repeat this process for the other figures in the row. After they construct the pattern, have the students determine what figure is needed to continue the pattern. Ask them to make the figure, place it in the dotted box, trace it, and color the pictures to match their cubes. Proceed to Row **B** and work with the students to identify and construct the pattern. Discuss the fact that the pattern can be described in terms of turning and/or flipping the figures. When the coloring activity is completed, distribute Activity Sheet 118 and allow students to continue the task.

Completing a Pattern (Activity 119–120)

Objectives:
> Using INTERLOCKING CUBES:
> 1. construct figures to match patterns
> 2. add a cube to a figure to complete a pattern

Materials:
> For each group of six students • One set of INTERLOCKING CUBES
>
> For each student   • Activity Sheets 119–120
>   • Crayons

Teacher Instructions:
> This lesson continues the activity of constructing patterns with connected figures and introduces the task of adding a cube to a beginning or other position within a pattern. The Activity Sheets involve the task of constructing partial figures, then filling in the missing cubes. The students should cover all shaded portions of each figure before they attempt to find the missing cube. Encourage the students to analyze the patterns and describe them in terms of color.

Classroom Activity:
> Divide each group into pairs, and ask one of each pair to remove two **red cubes** and the other to remove one **yellow cube** from the set of INTERLOCKING CUBES. Help the students join the cubes to form a length of three with an alternating pattern (RYR). Each student should then select one additional yellow cube from the set, adding each to the length so the pattern is continued. Discuss with the students the necessity of adding a yellow cube to each end of the length in order to continue the pattern. Each pair should then choose two other sets of cubes, four of one color and two of a second color. Work with them to make two lengths of three in alternating color patterns (XOX, XOX). Ask the students to determine what cube would be needed to join their two lengths and complete the color pattern.
>
> Distribute Activity Sheet 119 and ask the students to select two sets of INTERLOCKING CUBES, five each of two different colors. Each student should place a different colored cube on each shaded shape at the top of the sheet. Work with the students to identify the pattern in Row **A** (alternating colors), and encourage them to select the correct number and color of cubes needed to make the incomplete figure. After the students have constructed the partial figure and covered the picture, have them determine what cube should go in the unshaded space to continue the pattern, and place it in the space. Continue the process with Row **B** , working with the students to identify and construct the portion of the figure to the right of the unshaded space. Place the correct cube to the left of the unshaded space, and discuss what cube should be placed in the space to complete the pattern. Work with the students on the remaining exercises on the sheet. After they complete the sheet, distribute Activity Sheet 120 and allow students to continue the task.

Completing a Pattern (Activity 121–122)

Objectives:
Using INTERLOCKING CUBES:
1. construct figures and make a pattern
2. add a figure to complete a partial pattern

Materials:
For each group of six students • One set of INTERLOCKING CUBES

For each student   • Activity Sheets 121–122
                                        • Crayons

Teacher Instructions:
This lesson continues the activity of constructing patterns with connected figures. The Activity Sheets involve the task of constructing partial patterns and filling in the missing figure. The students should cover and construct all shaded portions of each pattern before attempting to determine the missing figure. Encourage the students to analyze the patterns, describing them in terms of the number of cubes of each color and the color patterns. Row **C** on Activity Sheet 122 requires twelve cubes of one color, so students will need to combine some sets to compete the exercise.

Classroom Activity:
Ask the students to select ten cubes of the same color from their set of INTERLOCKING CUBES and use the cubes to make five lengths of two cubes. Then, with the students working in pairs, have students combine their different colored lengths of two to make ten **two-by-two** squares. Ask the first student in each pair to begin a row of figures using one of the squares. Work with students to place the figure so that cubes of the same color are in the top row of the square. Ask the second student to place another square in the row, turning the figure until the color pattern has been reversed. (The top row contains cubes of the other color.) Continue the alternating pattern, asking the students to take turns placing the squares until all the figures have been placed in the row.

Distribute Activity Sheet 121 and ask the students to select two sets of ten INTERLOCKING CUBES, with each set a different color. Work with the students to identify the pattern in Row **A** (alternating colors), and encourage the students to select the correct numbers and colors of cubes needed to cover the shaded shapes. After they cover the pictures, help the students determine the which cube to place in the unshaded box to complete the pattern. Continue to Row **B** and encourage students to identify the pattern (different colors, different number of cubes). Each student should construct the two figures required for the pattern, then cover the pictures. After students determine what figure is needed to complete the pattern, the figure should be constructed and placed in the box. When the exercises are complete, allow the students to color the pictures to match their cubes; then distribute Activity Sheet 122 and allow students to work individually on the task.

Completing a Pattern (Activity 123–124)

Objectives:
> Using ATTRIBUTE BLOCKS:
> 1. construct a pattern to match a picture
> 2. add a shape to complete a pattern

Materials:
> For each group of six students • One set of ATTRIBUTE BLOCKS
>
> For each student   • Activity Sheets 123–124

Teacher Instructions:
> This activity uses ATTRIBUTE BLOCKS to continue the task of constructing and completing patterns. Both the initial activity and the Activity Sheets involve the construction of patterns based on the attribute of shape rather than color. The attribute of thickness should be ignored, since some patterns require both thick and thin blocks. Encourage the students to describe the patterns in terms of shape and position. Stress that replacing a block with a matching shape of different color does not affect the pattern. The geometric motion of turning is also incorporated in Activity Sheet 124 as a technique for defining a pattern.

Classroom Activity:
> Separate the ATTRIBUTE BLOCKS by size and return the small blocks to their containers. Ask each group of six to sort the large blocks by thickness, then have each student select a set of thick or thin blocks of the same shape. With the students working in pairs, ask them to take turns placing their blocks in a row, to creating an alternating pattern based upon shape and ignoring the attribute of color. Rearrange the students into groups of three and ask them to again take turns placing their blocks in a row, creating a new pattern based on three consecutive blocks of different shapes. Discuss the new patterns with the students, stressing that color and thickness are not used as attributes.
>
> Remove the small blocks from their containers and return the large blocks to their proper locations. Again ask the students to sort the blocks by thickness to provide each group of three students with fifteen blocks. Distribute Activity Sheets 123 and 124. Ask the students to decide which blocks they need to construct Row **A** on Activity Sheet 123. Two students in each group should then select the two sets of ATTRIBUTE BLOCKS needed and cover the pictures on the third student's sheet. After they finish the task, the third student should locate the block to complete the pattern, place it in the dotted box, and trace it. Rotate the tasks among the three students until all rows on the two sheets are completed. One group should begin at Row **B** on Activity Sheet 124, since five of the rectangle-shapes are required and groups must combine their blocks.

Completing a Pattern (Activity 125–126)

Objectives:
　　Using PATTERN BLOCKS:
　　　　1. construct a partial pattern to match a picture
　　　　2. add a shape to complete a pattern

Materials:
　　For each group of six students　• One set of PATTERN BLOCKS

　　For each student　　　　　　　• Activity Sheets 125–126
　　　　　　　　　　　　　　　　• Crayons

Teacher Instruction:
　　This lesson continues instruction on constructing and completing patterns, with PATTERN BLOCKS replacing ATTRIBUTE BLOCKS. Both the initial tasks and the Activity Sheets are intended to focus attention on constructing patterns based upon the attribute of shape rather than color. Encourage students to describe the patterns using shape alone. The geometric motions of flipping and/or turning are incorporated into the Activity Sheets to provide the additional criterion of position. Since some patterns on Activity Sheet 125 require a large number of blocks, the students may need to exchange shapes and work on different exercises to complete the sheet.

Classroom Activity:
　　With the students working in pairs, ask each student to remove two **hexagons** (yellow) and one **trapezoid** (red) from the set of PATTERN BLOCKS and place them in a row to make an alternating pattern (YRY). Ask the pairs which additional shape is needed to combine their two rows into a single row. Stress that the pattern in the two rows should not be rearranged, then have them form the longer row by sliding their cubes together and adding the correct shape (trapezoid). Repeat the activity, selecting other combinations of one and two blocks.

　　Distribute Activity Sheet 125 and ask the students how many of which shapes are needed to cover the pictures in Row **A**. Allow them to remove the appropriate number of blocks from the set of PATTERN BLOCKS and cover the pictures. Discuss with the students which block should be placed in the dotted box to complete the pattern, and allow time for the students to complete the tracing and coloring tasks. Students should then work simultaneously on the remaining two exercises, exchanging blocks to complete the activities. Work with the students who are constructing the pattern in Row **C**, pointing out that the block positions are a result of turning and/or flipping them. After completing the sheet, distribute Activity Sheet 126 and allow students to work individually to complete the activity.

Completing a Pattern (Activity 127–128)

Objectives:
Using ATTRIBUTE BLOCKS:
1. construct a partial pattern to match a picture
2. add a shape to complete a pattern

Materials:
For each group of six students • One set of ATTRIBUTE BLOCKS

For each student   • Activity Sheets 127–128
                                    • Crayons

Teacher Instructions:
This activity uses ATTRIBUTE BLOCKS to continue the task of constructing and completing patterns. Activity Sheet 127 involves patterns based on the attribute of color rather than shape or thickness, while Activity Sheet 128 concerns both color and shape. The attribute of thickness should be ignored, since some patterns will require both thick and thin blocks. In addition, because a number of shapes of the same color are needed for the patterns, the students should color the partial patterns before locating the block that completes that pattern.

Classroom Activity:
Remove the ATTRIBUTE BLOCKS from the container and sort them into two sets, large and small. With the students working in pairs, ask one pair to remove the six **large square-shapes**, the second pair to remove the six large **triangle-shapes**, and the third pair to remove the six **small rectangle-shapes** from the set of blocks. Ask each student in a pair to select the two shapes of the same color from their set and place the blocks in a combined row to form an alternating pattern with the two colors (OXOX). Repeat the activity using other combinations of colors and shapes. Encourage the students to explain and describe their constructions. If time permits, ask each group to use all three colors to create a new pattern based on three consecutive blocks of different colors.

Remove the remaining small blocks from their containers and return the large blocks to their proper locations. Distribute Activity Sheet 127 and work with the students to decide which blocks are needed for Row **A**. Before the students cover the pictures, continue to the other exercises on the sheet and discuss the pattern in each row. Then ask students to work in pairs on one row on the sheet. They should select the blocks needed, cover the four pictures, and color them to match the blocks. The students should then decide which block is needed to complete the pattern, place it in the dotted box, trace it, and color it correctly. The pairs should continue in this manner until all the rows on their sheets are complete. After distributing Activity Sheet 128, repeat the above sequence of activities, beginning with a discussion of the three exercises.

Sequences of Shapes (Activity 129–130)

Objectives:
Using PATTERN BLOCKS:
1. construct rows of shapes to make a pattern
2. add a row of shapes to continue a pattern

Materials:
For each group of six students • One set of PATTERN BLOCKS

For each student   • Activity Sheets 129–130
                                                    • Crayons

Teacher Instructions:
This lesson uses PATTERN BLOCKS to introduce the task of constructing a series of rows or sequences that create a pattern, then adding a row to continue the pattern. Initial activities require the students to work in pairs and introduce the concept of a pattern based on rows of blocks rather than individual blocks in a single row. Encourage students to verbalize the characteristics of the sequences and to select the correct number of blocks needed for each row before they do the actual construction. Since Activity Sheet 129 requires fifteen of the twenty-four rhombuses in the set of blocks, one group of three should work on that sheet while the other works on Activity Sheet 130. If a second set of PATTERN BLOCKS is available, students could work in pairs.

Classroom Activity:
Within each group of six, ask one pair of students to remove all the **hexagons** (yellow), the second pair all the **squares** (orange), and the third pair twelve **trapezoids** (red) from the set of PATTERN BLOCKS. Ask one student in each pair to place one block on the table, then ask the opposite student to use two blocks to build a second row directly beneath the first block.The first student should then make a third row of three blocks beneath the first two rows. The second student can then complete the task by building a row of four blocks. Discuss with the students the attributes of these rows of blocks and the pattern that is formed. If time permits, ask students to use two different shapes to build rows with an alternating pattern.

After distributing Activity Sheets 129 and 130, work with the students to decide what blocks are needed to cover the pictures on the two sheets. With the students working in groups of three, ask one trio to select the blocks for Activity Sheet 129 and the other trio to select the two sets of blocks for Activity Sheet 130. Each group should then build the sequences on one student's sheet, rotating the task of making each row among the group members. Encourage students to explain the attributes of the sequences (same shape, one more in each row) and to predict how many blocks are needed to build a row in the dotted box to continue the pattern. Rotate the tasks and the sets of blocks between the groups until all the sheets are completed, allowing time for students to trace the blocks and color the pictures.

Sequences of Shapes (Activity 131–132)

Objectives:
Using INTERLOCKING CUBES:
1. construct rows of cubes to make a pattern
2. add a row of cubes to continue a pattern

Materials:
For each group of six students • One set of INTERLOCKING CUBES

For each student   • Activity Sheets 131–132
                                     • Crayons

Teacher Instructions:
This lesson uses INTERLOCKING CUBES to further develop the concept of constructing rows or sequences that create a pattern, then continuing the pattern by building an additional row. The students should begin to realize that two patterns are involved in each activity, the one within each row and the one created by the sequence of rows. Class discussion should focus on the analysis of these two dimensions, and students should be encouraged to verbalize the properties of each component within the activity. The cubes should not be connected during the initial activities or on the Activity Sheets; later lessons will address connected patterns.

Classroom Activity:
Ask each student to select ten cubes of the same color from the set of INTERLOCKING CUBES. Review the activity of building rows to create a pattern, having the students construct one row with one cube; a second row with two cubes beneath the first row; then a third row with three cubes. Do not let them connect the cubes. As in previous lessons, encourage the students to analyze the pattern created by the rows and explain how many cubes would be needed to construct another row. Repeat the activity by asking the students to choose a second set of ten cubes and construct rows that use two colors in an alternating pattern. Again, discuss the pattern formed by the rows of cubes.

Distribute Activity Sheet 131 and ask students to select two sets of fifteen cubes, with each set a different color. Work with the students to construct the rows on the sheet using the different colored cubes. Encourage students to verbalize both the pattern in each row (alternating color) and the pattern formed by the rows of cubes (add one more cube of the opposite color). After completing the five rows, work with the students to decide how many cubes of each color are needed to make a row in the dotted box that continues the pattern created by the rows above. Allow time for the students to construct the pattern, trace the cubes, and color the pictures. Permit students to work independently on Activity Sheet 132.

Sequences of Figures (Activity 133–134)

Objectives:
> Using PATTERN BLOCKS:
>> 1. connect shapes to make a pattern
>> 2. add a figure to continue a pattern

Materials:
> For each group of six students • Two sets of PATTERN BLOCKS
>
> For each student   • Activity Sheets 133–134
>   • Crayons

Teacher Instructions:
> This lesson uses PATTERN BLOCKS to continue the tasks of constructing a series of rows or sequences that creates a pattern and adding a row that continues the pattern. The initial activities require the students to work in pairs and introduce the concept of a pattern based on rows of connected blocks. Continue to make the students aware that two patterns are involved in each activity, the one within each row and the one created by the sequences of rows. Class discussion should focus on the analysis of these two dimensions, and students should be encouraged to verbalize the properties of each component, including the number of blocks used to construct each row and the need to turn and/or flip the blocks. Since both Activity Sheets require a large number of triangles, two sets of blocks should be made available to each group.

Classroom Activity:
> Request each pair of students to select sixteen **rhombuses** (blue) from the sets of PATTERN BLOCKS. Ask the first student in each pair to place one block on the table, then ask the second student to select two blocks, combine them to make a length, and place the connected figure in a row directly under the first block. The first student should then use three blocks to make another length, and place it beneath the first two rows. Continue alternating the tasks until all the blocks are used. The students should then select sixteen **trapezoids** (red) from the sets of blocks and repeat the above activity. Stress to the students that joining the trapezoids requires turning and/or flipping every other block.
>
> After distributing Activity Sheets 133 and 134, discuss the patterns formed by the blocks in each row and emphasize the need to turn and/or flip the triangles to construct the rows. Have the students work in groups of three. Ask one trio to select the blocks needed for Activity Sheet 133 and the other to select the blocks needed for Activity Sheet 134. (Do not select the blocks needed to continue the pattern in dotted boxes.) Ask each group to use one student's sheet to cover the sequences, rotating the task of making each row among the group members. Then work with each trio to determine how many blocks are needed to make a row that continues the pattern, and allow time for students to construct the figure, trace the blocks, and color the pictures. Continue the activity until all sheets are complete.

Sequences of Figures (Activity 135–136)

Objectives:
Using INTERLOCKING CUBES:
1. construct figures to make a partial pattern
2. construct a figure to complete a pattern

Materials:
For each group of six students • One set of INTERLOCKING CUBES

For each student   • Activity Sheets 135–136
                                        • Crayons

Teacher Instructions:
This lesson uses INTERLOCKING CUBES to introduce the tasks of constructing a series of rows or sequences to create a partial pattern, then adding a row that completes the pattern. Continue to make the students aware that two patterns are involved in the activity: the one within each row, and the one created by the sequence of rows. Class discussion should focus on the analysis of these two dimensions, and students should be encouraged to verbalize the properties of each component, including the color pattern and the number of cubes used to construct each figure. While the students work on completing the pattern formed by the rows, encourage them to think about two possibilities: adding a cube to the length just before the dotted box, or removing a cube from the length right after the dotted box.

Classroom Activity:
With the students working in pairs, ask one student in each pair to select twenty cubes of one color and the second student twenty of a different color from the sets of INTERLOCKING CUBES. Combine the two selected sets and ask the first student in each pair to place one cube on the table. Have the second student select two different colors of cubes, make a length of two, and place it directly under the first cube so that the color of the first cube in each row is the same. The first student should then use three cubes to make another length to continue the pattern, placing it beneath the first two rows. Stress to the students that each row contains an alternating pattern based upon color, and that the pattern formed by the rows involves adding a cube of the opposite color to each length. Continue the activity until all the cubes are used.

After distributing Activity Sheet 135, allow the students to work in pairs, using their two sets of cubes to construct figures that match the pictures on the sheet. Discuss the partial pattern formed by the rows of cubes. Work with the students to decide what cubes they will need to construct a figure to place in the dotted box, completing the partial pattern formed by the other rows. Stress that they should compare the lengths just before and after the dotted box. Each pair should then construct the length, trace the cubes, and color the pictures. After the students complete the sheet, distribute Activity Sheet 136 and allow them to continue the tasks.

Sequences of Shapes (Activity 137–138)

Objectives:
>   Using PATTERN BLOCKS:
>   1. make rows of shapes to create a partial pattern
>   2. add a row of shapes to complete a pattern

Materials:
>   For each group of six students • One set of PATTERN BLOCKS
>
>   For each student   • Activity Sheets 137–138
>   • Crayons

Teacher Instructions:
>   This is the last of a series of activities involving the identification of a pattern created by rows or sequences of figures. The lesson uses PATTERN BLOCKS to continue the task of constructing a series of rows to create a partial pattern, then adding a row that completes the pattern formed by the sequences of shapes. Continue to make the students aware that two patterns are involved in each activity: the one within each row, and the one created by the sequence of rows. Class discussion should again focus on analyzing these two dimensions. Encourage the students to verbalize the properties of each component, including the number of blocks used to construct each row and the need for turning and/or flipping some of the blocks to create the patterns.

Classroom Activity:
>   Have the students work in groups of three. Ask one student in each group to remove twelve **trapezoids** (red), another twelve **rhombuses** (blue), and the third six **hexagons** (yellow) from the set of PATTERN BLOCKS. Work with each group to construct a row of shapes with the following pattern: TRHTRH. Next, ask the students to arrange a row of five blocks in a pattern that could be placed above the first constructed row (TRHTR). Continue the process until only a trapezoid remains, reducing the number of blocks in each row by one.
>
>   Distribute Activity Sheet 137 and have the students working in pairs. Ask one student in the pair to select eight **rhombuses** (blue) and the other student eight **triangles** (green) from the set of PATTERN BLOCKS. Discuss the patterns formed by each row with the students (shapes and positions), stressing that the patterns in each row include some turned and/or flipped shapes. Allow time for the students to cover the shapes on the sheet, then work with them to construct the row that completes the pattern formed by the sequences. As some pairs are completing their sheets, distribute Activity Sheet 138 and work with other pairs to begin the tasks on that sheet.

Paper Folding (Activity 139–140)

Objectives:
Using PATTERN BLOCKS:
1. match blocks to pictures of shapes
2. make a figure to match an unfolded pattern

Materials:
For each group of six students • One set of PATTERN BLOCKS

For each student   • Activity Sheets 139–140
                                     • Crayons

Teacher Instructions:
This lesson begins a series of activities using PATTERN BLOCKS to introduce some elementary aspects of symmetry. The initial tasks focus on the activity of placing one block on top of another, then flipping one of them along a side to create a figure that is symmetrical about a line. Before beginning the lesson, tape several combinations of two matching blocks together so students can see the end product of this particular geometric motion. Encourage the students to predict the shape of the figure that will be formed when the two blocks have been "unfolded."

Classroom Activity:
Begin by taping two **trapezoids** (red) together to form a hexagon, then fold the taped figure so that one block is on top of the other. Ask each student to select two **trapezoids** from the set of PATTERN BLOCKS and to place the blocks in the same "folded" position. Discuss with the students what figure would be formed if the taped trapezoids were unfolded, and ask them to select a block from the set that they think would match the shape of the unfolded trapezoids (hexagon). Encourage the students to "unfold" their two trapezoids and compare the resulting figure to the block they selected. Repeat the activity, using two **triangles** (green) that unfold to form a rhombus.

After distributing Activity Sheet 139, ask the students to select four **trapezoids** (red) for the exercise at the top of the sheet. Work with the students to place one block on the shaded shape to the left and a second block on top of the first block. Encourage the students to verbalize how they should move the top block to match the unfolding action. (The top block must be flipped along its short vertical side.) Next, ask the students to place their other two blocks in the correct positions on the figure to the right, unfold the two blocks on the left, and compare the results. Work with the students again to select four **rhombuses** (blue) from the set of blocks and repeat the process for the bottom exercise on the sheet. Begin by covering the left shape with two blocks, then placing the other two blocks in their correct positions on the right figure, and, finally, unfolding the blocks on the left to verify the prediction. After students complete the sheet, distribute Activity Sheet 140 and allow them to work individually on the exercises.

Paper Folding (Activity 141–142)

Objectives:
>Using PATTERN BLOCKS:
>1. trace blocks and cut out shapes
>2. make a figure to match an unfolded pattern

Materials:
>For each group of six students • One set of PATTERN BLOCKS
>
>For each student   • Activity Sheets 141–142
>   • Folded paper
>   • Scissors and crayons

Teacher Instructions:
>This lesson continues to use PATTERN BLOCKS to develop elementary ideas of symmetry. The initial tasks require students to place a block on a folded piece of paper with one side along the folded edge, trace the block, cut out the shape, and unfold the paper to create a new figure that is symmetrical about the fold. Continue encouraging the students to predict the shape of the figure that will be formed when the pieces of paper are unfolded. A template, if available, might facilitate the tracing process. After completing the activity, collect the cutouts and save them for Activity 143–144.

Classroom Activity:
>Distribute folded pieces of paper and scissors to students, then ask each to select two **hexagons** (yellow) from the set of PATTERN BLOCKS. Have them place one side of one hexagon along the folded edge of the paper and trace the block. The students should then use their hexagons to make a figure which they think will match the figure formed after the traced shape is cut out and the paper unfolded. When the constructions are complete, allow the students to cut out the shape, unfold the paper, and verify their predictions. If time permits, allow them to select other blocks and repeat the activity.
>
>After distributing Activity Sheet 141, ask the students to select four **rhombuses** (tan) to use in the top exercise on the sheet. Work with the students to place one block on the shaded shape at the left and a second block on top of the first one. Ask the students to place two blocks on the "opened paper" to the right so that they will match the figure formed when the cutout paper is unfolded. Encourage the students to verbalize how the top block moves to match the unfolding action. (It must be flipped along vertical side.) Help the students unfold the two blocks on the left, and compare the results. Work with the students again to select four **squares** (orange) from the set of blocks, and repeat the process for the other exercise on the sheet. Begin by covering the left shape with two blocks, then placing the other two blocks in the correct position on the right figure, and, finally, unfolding the blocks on the left to verify the prediction. After completing the sheet, distribute Activity Sheet 142 and allow students to work individually on the remaining exercises.

Paper Folding (Activity 143–144)

Objectives:

Using PATTERN BLOCKS:
1. trace blocks and cut out shapes
2. find a shape to match a folded pattern

Materials:

For each group of six students • One set of PATTERN BLOCKS

For each student
- Activity Sheets 143–144
- Cutouts from the previous lesson
- Crayons

Teacher Instructions:

This lesson uses PATTERN BLOCKS to continue developing elementary ideas of symmetry by reversing the tasks of the previous activities. The initial tasks use the cutout figures from the last lesson to predict the shape that will result from folding a piece of paper (figure) instead of unfolding it. Students should continue to work on describing the shapes of the figures formed when the pieces of paper are folded. If a template is available, it might facilitate the tracing process.

Classroom Activity:

Distribute the folded paper cutout figures made in the last activity. Ask each student to first unfold the paper, then locate two blocks that will cover the cutout. Discuss with the students how the two blocks should be moved to create a figure that will match the figure formed when the paper is folded. (One block must be flipped along a vertical edge and placed on top of the other block.) Allow time for the students to flip the block, then fold the paper and compare results. If other figures were cut out in the last lesson, use them to repeat the above procedure.

After distributing Activity Sheet 143, ask the students to select four **squares** (orange) to use in the top exercise on the sheet. Work with the students to place two blocks on the shaded figure on the right. Discuss with them what shape will be created if the paper on the right is folded along the dotted line, then allow them to place a block in the correct position on the "folded paper" pictured to the left. Encourage the students to explain how the blocks on the right figure must be moved to match the folding action. (One block must be flipped along a vertical side.) Students should then fold the two blocks on the right and compare the result to the left figure. Work with the students again as they select four **triangles** (green) from the set of blocks and repeat the process for the exercise at the bottom. Have the students first cover the right figure with two blocks, then place the two other blocks in the correct position on the "folded paper" pictured to the left, and fold the blocks on the right to verify their prediction. After the students complete the exercises, distribute Activity Sheet 144 and allow students to continue work individually.

72

CLASSIFICATIONS

Classifying—Color and Shape (Activity 145–146)

Objectives:
 Using ATTRIBUTE BLOCKS:
  1. sort blocks by size
  2. classify blocks according to color and shape

Materials:
 For each group of six students • One set of ATTRIBUTE BLOCKS

 For each student • Activity Sheets 145–146
  • Crayons

Teacher Instructions:
 This lesson uses ATTRIBUTE BLOCKS to introduce the task of classifying blocks by two attributes: shape and color. Both the initial activities and the Activity Sheets present classification as a two-step process. Once the blocks have been separated by size, ask the students to create a set by sorting the blocks by shape, then asked to sort the newly created set by color. After the students have completed the first block sorting, encourage them to describe the properties of their sets. (They are the same shape and size, but different colors and thicknesses). During the second sorting, point out that the blocks are not sorted by thickness and the students may use both thick and thin blocks in the same set.

Classroom Activity:
 Separate the large and small ATTRIBUTE BLOCKS and return the small blocks to their containers. Ask each group of six students to sort the large blocks by shape. With the students working in pairs, ask the first pair to select the **hexagon-shapes**, the second pair the **square-shapes,** and the third pair the **rectangle-shapes**. Hold up a **red square-shape** and determine which pair of students has a set of blocks of the same shape. Ask each student in the pair to locate a block that is also the same color as your block, and stress that either a thick or thin block can be used. Repeat the activity using the **yellow hexagon-shape** and the **blue rectangle-shape.**

 Remove the small blocks from their containers and return the large blocks to their proper locations. Distribute Activity Sheets 145 and 146, hold up a **small square-shape,** and ask the students to select the same shape from their sets. (The color of the shapes can differ.) Discuss with the students the shape of the block needed to cover the pictured shape in Exercise **A** on Sheet 145, and determine which students have a block that is the correct color. (Two students should have correct blocks.) One of the students should place the block on the picture and the other student should complete the exercise by placing the corresponding block in the dotted box. Allow the students to continue working in pairs, taking turns selecting blocks to cover the pictures, locating the corresponding blocks to place in the dotted boxes, then completing the exercises on both sheets.

Classifying—Color and Shape (Activity 147–148)

Objectives:
> Using ATTRIBUTE BLOCKS:
> 1. sort blocks by size
> 2. classify blocks according to color and shape

Materials:
> For each group of six students • One set of ATTRIBUTE BLOCKS
>
> For each student   • Activity Sheets 147–148
>   • Crayons

Teacher Instructions:
> This lesson uses ATTRIBUTE BLOCKS, continuing the task of classifying blocks by two attributes: shape and color. It differs from the previous lesson in that it requires students to construct a set using "different color" as an attribute. Classification is again presented as a two-step process, first sorting the blocks by shape, then classifying the shapes according to color. After the students have completed the first block sorting, continue encouraging them to describe the properties of their sets. (The blocks are the same shape and size, but different colors and thicknesses.)

Classroom Activity:
> Separate the large and small ATTRIBUTE BLOCKS and return the small blocks to their containers. Ask each group of six students to sort the large blocks by shape. With the students working in pairs, ask the first pair to select the **rectangle-shapes**, the second pair the **square-shapes**, and the third pair the **triangle-shapes**. Hold up a **blue rectangle-shape** and determine which pair has a set of blocks of the same shape. Encourage the other pairs of students to verbalize how their sets are different. (They have the wrong number of sides; the sides are all the same length, etc.) Then ask students in the first pair to locate in their set all the blocks that have a color that is different from your block. Stress that either a thick or thin block can be used. Discuss the properties of this new set with the students, emphasizing the attributes of shape and color. Repeat the activity using the other sets of shapes.
>
> Remove the small blocks from their containers and return the large blocks to their proper locations. Distribute Activity Sheets 147 and 148, hold up a **small square-shape,** and ask each student to select the same shape from the set. (The color of the shapes may differ.) Discuss with the students the shape of the block needed to cover the pictured shape in Exercise **A** on Sheet 147, and determine which students have a block that is the correct color (yellow). Then ask which students have a block of the same shape, but a different color. One of the students should then place the correct block on the picture on the left and another student should complete the exercise by placing the appropriate block in the dotted box (a red or yellow square-shape). Allow the students to work individually on the remaining exercises on both sheets.

Classifying—Color and Shape (Activity 149–150)

Objectives:
Using ATTRIBUTE BLOCKS:
1. sort blocks by size
2. classify blocks according to color and shape

Materials:
For each group of six students   • One set of ATTRIBUTE BLOCKS

For each student   • Activity Sheets 149–150
                                     • Crayons

Teacher Instructions:
This lesson uses ATTRIBUTE BLOCKS, continuing the task of classifying blocks by two attributes: shape and color. Since it requires students to construct a set using "different shape" instead of "different color" as an attribute, it differs from the previous lesson. Classification is again presented as a two-step process, first sorting the blocks by color, then classifying them by shape. After the students have completed the first block sorting, continue encouraging them to describe the properties of their sets. (They are the same color and size, but different shapes and thicknesses.)

Classroom Activity:
After separating the ATTRIBUTE BLOCKS by size, return the small blocks to their containers. Ask each group of six students to sort the large blocks by color. Then, with the students working in pairs, ask the first pair to select the red blocks from their set, the second pair the blue, and the third pair the yellow. Hold up a **red hexagon-shape** and determine which pair of students has a set of blocks of the same color. Encourage the other pairs to verbalize how their sets of blocks differ. (They are the wrong color; there are other shapes in their set; etc.) Then ask students in the first pair to locate all the blocks in their set with a different shape from your block. Stress that both thick and thin blocks can be used. Discuss the properties of this new set with the students, emphasizing the comparative attributes of color and shape (similarity and difference). Repeat the activity using the other two colors.

Remove the small blocks from their containers and return the large blocks to their proper locations. Distribute Activity Sheets 149 and 150; discuss with the students the shape and color of the block needed to cover the pictured shape in Exercise **A** on Sheet 149, and ask one student to select the correct block. Then ask other students to select blocks with the same color but different shapes. Discuss that more than one shape can be used to complete the exercise. (There are four possible choices.) Students should then work individually on the sheets, placing the correct block on the left-hand picture in each exercise, then completing the exercises by placing the appropriate blocks in the dotted boxes. (The blocks should be the same colors but different shapes). Continue to stress that answers will differ from student to student depending on their selection of shapes.

Classifying—Color and Shape (Activity 151–152)

Objectives:
> Using ATTRIBUTE BLOCKS:
> 1. sort blocks by size
> 2. classify blocks according to color and shape

Materials:

For each group of six students	• One set of ATTRIBUTE BLOCKS
For each student	• Activity Sheets 151–152
	• Crayons

Teacher Instructions:
> This lesson is the last in a series of activities involving the task of classifying ATTRIBUTE BLOCKS by two attributes: shape and color. It differs from the previous lesson since it requires students to construct a set using the attributes of "different shape" and "different color." Classification is again presented as a two-step process, first sorting by color, then by shape. After the students have completed the first block sorting, continue encouraging them to describe the properties of their sets. (They are the same color and size, but different shapes and thicknesses.)

Classroom Activity:
> After separating the ATTRIBUTE BLOCKS by size, return the small blocks to their containers. Ask each group of six students to sort the large blocks by color. Then, with the students working in pairs, ask the first pair to select the red blocks from their set, the second pair the blue, and the third pair the yellow. Hold up a **red rectangle-shape** and ask each pair of students to make a set consisting of all the blocks with a shape different from your block. Stress that different thicknesses and colors can be used to construct the set. Then determine which pairs have constructed sets that also differ from your block by color. Discuss the properties of these new sets with the students, emphasizing the attributes of color and shape (both are different). Repeat the activity using the other two colors.

> Remove the small blocks from their containers and return the large blocks to their proper locations. Distribute Activity Sheets 151 and 152, discuss with the students the block needed to cover the pictured shape in Exercise **A** on Sheet 151, and ask one student to select the correct color block (blue). Then ask each student to select a block with a different color and different shape. Discuss the students' choices, and stress that more than one shape and color can be used to complete the exercise. Students should then work individually on the sheets, placing the correct block on the left-hand picture in each exercise, then completing the exercise by placing the appropriate block in the dotted box. (The block should be a different color and shape.) Continue to stress that answers will differ from student to student.

Classifying—Color and Shape (Activity 153–154)

Objectives:
Using INTERLOCKING CUBES:
1. construct figures to match pictures
2. classify figures according to color and shape

Materials:
For each group of six students • One set of INTERLOCKING CUBES

For each student   • Activity Sheets 153–154
                                 • Crayons

Teacher Instructions:
This lesson continues the task of classifying objects by the attributes of shape and color. Using INTERLOCKING CUBES instead of ATTRIBUTE BLOCKS allows the concept to be extended to more complex figures. Later lessons will introduce sorting tasks based on differences as well as similarities. Continue encouraging discussion that focuses on the attributes of the figures and begin to emphasize the attributes or properties of the entire set of figures, rather than comparing individual pieces within the set. (*All* the figures are the same shape; or *all* the figures are the same color.) Since the figures constructed for this lesson will also be needed in the next two lessons, you may choose to leave them intact at the conclusion of the activity.

Classroom Activity:
Ask each student to select three sets of four INTERLOCKING CUBES, with each set a different color. Hold up a **T-shaped figure** made of four cubes and ask the students to construct three figures of the same shape with their sets. After the students have completed the construction task, have them compare figures to determine whether any students have figures that are the same color. Students should then make sets of figures by collecting all the figures of the same color. Encourage the students to compare sets and to verbalize the differences between them using the attribute of color. (All the figures are the same shape, but the sets differ in color.)

Distribute Activity Sheet 153 and allow the students to work in pairs. Ask each pair to select two sets of ten INTERLOCKING CUBES. Allow time for each group to construct the figures at the top of the sheet (two of each figure). Discuss the attributes of the figures with the students, emphasizing differences and similarities in shape and color within each group. Ask one student in each pair to place the correct figure on the picture in Exercise **A** on one student's copy of sheet 153. Then ask the other student in each pair to locate a figure that could be placed in the dotted box. (It should have the same shape and color.) Reverse the roles of the students, having one student in each pair locate the two figures needed to complete Exercise **A** on the other student's sheet. Allow students to continue working in pairs to finish the exercises on the sheet, then continue with Activity Sheet 154.

Classifying—Color and Shape (Activity 155–156)

Objectives:
>   Using INTERLOCKING CUBES:
>   1. construct figures to match pictures
>   2. classify figures according to color and shape

Materials:
>   For each group of six students • One set of INTERLOCKING CUBES
>
>   For each student   • Activity Sheets 155–156
>   • Crayons

Teacher Instructions:
>   This activity uses INTERLOCKING CUBES to continue the task of classifying objects by the attributes of shape and color. The lesson introduces sorting tasks based upon differences as well as similarities. Continue to encourage discussion involving the attributes of the figures and emphasize the attributes or properties of the entire set of figures, rather than comparing individual pieces within the set. (*All* the figures are the same shape; *all* the figures are the same color, etc.) The Activity Sheets require the same figures as those used in the previous lesson. If the figures were saved, the construction portion of the task can be omitted. Since these figures will also be needed in the next lesson, you may again choose to leave them intact at the conclusion of the activity.

Classroom Activity:
>   Ask each student to select three sets of four INTERLOCKING CUBES, with each set a different color. Hold up an **L-shaped figure** made of four cubes and ask the students to construct three figures of the same shape with their cubes. After they complete the construction task, students should then make sets of figures by collecting all figures with the same color. Ask one student to hold up a figure from one of the sets and ask other students whether their sets contain different colored figures. Encourage the students to compare sets and to verbalize the color differences between them.
>
>   Distribute Activity Sheet 155 and allow the students to work in pairs. Ask each group to select two sets of ten INTERLOCKING CUBES, or use figures from the previous lesson. Allow time for each pair to construct the figures at the top of the sheet (two of each figure). Discuss the attributes of the figures with the students, emphasizing differences and similarities in shape and color within each group. Ask the first student in each pair to place the correct figure on the picture in Exercise **A** on the second student's sheet. Then ask the second student to find the figure that should be placed in the dotted box. (It should have the same shape, but a different color.) Reverse the roles of the students and have the second student locate the two figures needed for Exercise **B** on the first student's sheet. Allow students to work in pairs to complete the exercises on their sheets, then continue with Activity Sheet 156.

Classifying—Color and Shape (Activity 157–158)

Objectives:
  Using INTERLOCKING CUBES:
   1. construct figures to match pictures
   2. classify figures according to color and shape

Materials:
  For each group of six students • One set of INTERLOCKING CUBES

  For each student   • Activity Sheets 157–158
                                      • Crayons

Teacher Instructions:
  This lesson is the last in a series of activities that uses INTERLOCKING CUBES to classify objects by the attributes of shape and color. As in the previous lesson, the sorting tasks are based upon differences as well as similarities. The Activity Sheets require the students to classify by different shape and different color. Continue to encourage discussion based upon the attributes of the figures, emphasizing the attributes or properties of the entire set of figures, rather than comparing individual pieces within the set. (*All* the figures are the same shape; or *all* the figures are the same color.) Since the Activity Sheets employ the same figures as those used in the earlier lessons, if the figures were saved, the construction task can be omitted.

Classroom Activity:
  Ask each student to select four sets of four INTERLOCKING CUBES, with each set a different color. Hold up an **L-shaped** and a **T-shaped** figure. Ask the students to construct two figures of each shape with their cubes. After the students have completed the construction task, they should make sets of figures by collecting all figures that are the same color and shape. Ask one student to hold up a figure from one of the sets and ask other students whether they can locate a set that contains figures of a different color and shape. Encourage the students to compare sets and to verbalize the color and shape differences between them. Repeat the activity as time permits.

  Distribute Activity Sheet 157 and allow the students to work in pairs. Ask each group to select two sets of ten INTERLOCKING CUBES, or use the figures from the previous lesson. Allow time for each pair to construct the figures at the top of the sheet (two of each figure). Discuss the attributes of the figures with the students, emphasizing differences and similarities in shape and color within each group. Ask the first student in each pair to place the correct figure on the picture in Exercise **A** on the second student's sheet; then have the second student find the figure that should be placed in the dotted box. (It should be a different shape and color). Reverse the roles of the two students and have the second student locate the two figures needed for Exercise **B** on the first student's sheet. Allow students to work in pairs to complete the exercises on the sheets, then continue with Activity Sheet 158.

79

Classifying—Color, Shape, and Size (Activity 159–160)

Objectives:
Using ATTRIBUTE BLOCKS:
1. sort blocks by thickness
2. classify blocks according to color, shape, and size

Materials:

For each group of six students	• One set of ATTRIBUTE BLOCKS
For each student	• Activity Sheets 159–160
	• Crayons

Teacher Instructions:
This lesson uses ATTRIBUTE BLOCKS to extend the earlier task of using two attributes to classify blocks to using three attributes: shape, color, and size. Both the initial activities and the Activity Sheets present classification as a multistep process. After the students divide the blocks by thickness, they are asked to create sets by sorting the blocks according to shape, with the resulting sets containing both large and small shapes. When the students complete each block sorting, they should be encouraged to describe the properties of their sets using the attributes of size, shape, and color. The final task requires students to select blocks with the same shape and color but a different size.

Classroom Activity:
Ask each group of six students to sort the ATTRIBUTE BLOCKS by thickness, then by shape to create ten sets, each containing both large and small shapes. Assign the sets so that two students have the thick and thin **hexagon-shapes,** two students the thick and thin **circle-shapes,** and two students the thick and thin **triangle-shapes.** Hold up a **large red hexagon-shape** and determine which students have the sets of blocks of the same shape. Ask these students to locate a block with the same color and size as your block. Then ask them to find a block the same color but a different size. Repeat the activity using the **large** and **small yellow triangle-shapes** and **blue circle-shapes.**

Distribute Activity Sheet 159 and discuss the shape, color, and size of the block needed to cover the pictured shape in Exercise **A** with the students. Determine which students have a block with the correct attributes. (Two students should have correct blocks.) After these students place the blocks on the sheets, ask the other students to find blocks with the same shape and color but a different size. Once they have placed the correct blocks in the dotted box, work with the group to find the shapes needed to complete Exercise **B.** Distribute Activity Sheet 160 and have the students continue the task of locating blocks that are the same shape and color but a different size. Allow time to complete the tracing and coloring activities on each sheet.

Classifying—Color, Shape, and Size (Activity 161–162)

Objectives:
Using ATTRIBUTE BLOCKS:
1. sort blocks by thickness
2. classify blocks according to color, shape, and size

Materials:

For each group of six students • One set of ATTRIBUTE BLOCKS

For each student   • Activity Sheets 161–162
                            • Crayons

Teacher Instructions:
This lesson uses ATTRIBUTE BLOCKS to continue the task of classifying blocks by three attributes: shape, color, and size. Both the initial activities and the Activity Sheets present classification as a multistep process. After the students have divided the blocks by thickness, they are asked to create sets by sorting the blocks by shape. The resulting sets will contain both large and small shapes. Once they have completed each block sorting, the students should be encouraged to describe the properties of their sets using size, shape, and color. The final task requires students to find blocks that have the same shape, but a different color and size. This task introduces the possibility of more than one correct response for each exercise.

Classroom Activity:
Ask each group of six students to sort the ATTRIBUTE BLOCKS by thickness, then by shape to create ten sets, each containing both large and small shapes. Assign the sets so that two students have the thick and thin **rectangle-shapes**, two students the thick and thin **circle-shapes,** and two students the thick and thin **triangle-shapes**. Hold up a **large blue rectangle-shape** and determine which students have the sets of blocks of the same shape. Ask these students to locate a block with the same color and size as your block. Then ask them to find a block that is the same color but a different size. Finally, ask the students to locate a block that is the same shape but a different color and different size. Repeat the activity using the **large** and **small red triangle-shapes** and **yellow circle-shapes**.

Distribute Activity Sheet 161 and discuss the shape, color, and size of the block needed to cover the pictured shape in Exercise **A** with the students. Determine which students have a block with the correct attributes. (Two students should have the correct blocks.) After these students have located the blocks, work with the other students to find blocks with the correct attributes that could be placed in the dotted box. (They should be the same shape but a different color and size.) Then work with the students to find the blocks needed to complete Exercise **B**. Distribute Activity Sheet 162 and allow students to continue the task of locating blocks for each exercise. Allow time to complete the tracing and coloring activities.

Classifying—Color, Shape, and Size (Activity 163–164)

Objectives:

Using ATTRIBUTE BLOCKS:
1. sort blocks by thickness
2. classify blocks according to color, shape, and size

Materials:

For each group of six students • One set of ATTRIBUTE BLOCKS

For each student   • Activity Sheets 163–164
                                     • Crayons

Teacher Instructions:

This lesson uses ATTRIBUTE BLOCKS to continue the task of classifying blocks by three attributes: shape, color, and size. Once again, both the initial activities and the Activity Sheets present classification as a multistep process. In addition, the activities allow several different correct answers for each task. After the students have divided the blocks by thickness, they should work in groups of three on the task of selecting blocks with the appropriate attributes. Once they have completed each block sorting, continue encouraging them to describe the properties of their sets using the attributes of size, shape, and color. The final task requires students to find blocks that are the same color but a different shape and size.

Classroom Activity:

Ask the students to sort the ATTRIBUTE BLOCKS by thickness and assign the sets to groups of three students. (Each group should have thirty blocks.) Hold up a **large blue hexagon-shape** and ask a student in each group to find a block that is the same shape, color, and size. Ask the other students in each group to locate a block with the same shape but a different color and size. Then ask all the students to locate a block of the same color but with a different shape and size. Encourage the students to verbalize and compare the attributes of the various blocks. Continue to review as time permits, using various combinations of attributes (shape, color, and size).

Distribute Activity Sheet 163 and discuss the shape, color, and size of the block needed to cover the pictured shape in Exercise **A** with the students. Ask one student in each group to find a block with the correct attributes and place it on the picture. After they have placed the blocks on the pictures, work with the other students to find a block with the same color but a different shape and size. (There are several choices.) After they identify blocks with the correct attributes to place in the dotted boxes, work with the groups to identify and select blocks to complete Exercise **B**. Distribute Activity Sheet 164 and continue the tasks. Allow time for students to complete the tracing and coloring activities on each sheet.

Classifying—Color, Shape, and Size (Activity 165–166)

Objectives:
Using ATTRIBUTE BLOCKS:
1. sort blocks by thickness
2. classify blocks according to color, shape, and size

Materials:
For each group of six students • One set of ATTRIBUTE BLOCKS

For each student   • Activity Sheets 165–166
                                • Crayons

Teacher Instructions:
This lesson concludes the series of activities using ATTRIBUTE BLOCKS to develop the ability to classify by three attributes: shape, color, and size. Once again, both the initial activities and the Activity Sheets present classification as a multistep process, with students being asked to find blocks that differ by shape, color, and size from a given block. After dividing the blocks into thick and thin shapes, the students should work in groups of three on the task of selecting blocks with the appropriate attributes. Continue encouraging the students to describe their sets' properties after each sorting of the blocks. Again, there is the possibility of more than one correct response to each exercise.

Classroom Activity:
Ask the students to sort the ATTRIBUTE BLOCKS by thickness and assign the resulting sets of blocks to groups of three students. (Each group should have thirty blocks.) Hold up a **large yellow circle-shape** and ask one student from each group to find a block with the same shape, the same color, and the same size. Ask the other students in the groups to locate a block with the same shape but a different color and different size. Then ask all students in the groups to locate a block with a different shape, different color, and different size. Encourage the students to verbalize and compare the attributes of the various blocks. Continue the review, using various combinations of attributes (shape, color, and size) as time permits.

After distributing Activity Sheet 165, discuss with the students the shape, color, and size of the block needed to cover the pictured shape in Exercise **A**. Ask one student in each group to find a block with all of the correct attributes. Work with the other students to help them find blocks with a different shape, different color, and different size than the first block. (There are several choices.) After they select blocks with the correct attributes to place in the dotted box, continue working with the groups to find the blocks to complete Exercise **B**. Distribute Activity Sheet 166 and help the students continue locating blocks that are a different size, color, and shape than the one pictured in each exercise. Allow time for individual students to complete the tracing and coloring activities on each sheet.

Grouping by Shape (Activity 167–168)

Objectives:

Using ATTRIBUTE BLOCKS:
1. classify blocks by shape and size
2. group blocks according to common attributes

Materials:

For each group of six students • One set of ATTRIBUTE BLOCKS

For each student   • Activity Sheets 167–168
                                                   • Crayons

Teacher Instructions:

This lesson uses ATTRIBUTE BLOCKS to introduce a series of activities that continues to explore the classification of blocks according to more than one attribute. Both the initial activities and the Activity Sheets present the task of forming a group of blocks with the common attributes of shape and size while ignoring the attributes of color and thickness. After the students sort the blocks according to the attributes and combine them to form sets of six, encourage them to describe the properties of their sets. (All blocks in the set are the same size and shape but different colors and different thicknesses.) Since only four students will be able to work simultaneously on the Activity Sheet exercises, some students will need to wait to use the set of blocks. Alternatively, the students could sort the block set by thickness prior to beginning the Activity Sheets. This would reduce each individual's set to three instead of six blocks.

Classroom Activity:

Hold up a **large blue hexagon-shape** and ask each student in the group to find a block that is the same shape and size, but not necessarily the same color. Then ask the group to combine their selected blocks to form a new set and discuss the properties of that set using the attributes of size, shape, and color (same shape and size, but different colors). Repeat the activity as time permits, using blocks of different shapes, sizes, and colors, and encourage the students to verbalize and compare the attributes of each set formed.

After distributing Activity Sheet 167, discuss with the students the shape and size of the block needed to cover the pictured shape in Exercise **A**. Stress that the color and thickness of the blocks may vary from student to student. Ask each student in the group to find a block with the correct attributes that could be placed in the box. Next, work with the students to identify and select blocks that can be used to complete Exercise **B**. Distribute Activity Sheet 168 and allow the students to continue the task of locating blocks with the same shape and size as the one pictured in each exercise. Allow time for individual students to complete the tracing and coloring activities.

Grouping by Shape (Activity 169–170)

Objectives:

Using PATTERN BLOCKS:
1. classify blocks by shape
2. group blocks according to a common attribute

Materials:

For each group of six students • One set of PATTERN BLOCKS

For each student   • Activity Sheets 169–170
                                                • Crayons

Teacher Instructions:

This lesson uses PATTERN BLOCKS to continue exploring the classification of blocks and the formation of sets based upon the common property of shape. After sorting the blocks based on this attribute and combining them into sets, encourage the students to describe their set's properties using the attributes of shape and number of sides. Since the blocks are color-coded and grouping activities can be based solely on this attribute, direct the students' attention toward discussing the attributes of the shapes of the various blocks, e.g., the number of sides, the size of the angles, the length of the sides.

Classroom Activity:

Working with pairs of students, ask each student to remove handsful of blocks from the set of PATTERN BLOCKS until the set has been roughly divided among the three pairs in each group. Hold up a **hexagon** (yellow). Ask one student in each pair to locate the same block in their set and the other to choose another block with the same shape and place it with the block chosen by the first student. Continue the process until all hexagons have been chosen and three sets of hexagons have been created. Ask the students to compare their sets in terms of the number of blocks. Repeat the activity, using different shapes as time permits. Encourage the students to verbalize and compare the attributes of the sets formed.

After distributing Activity Sheet 169, discuss with the students the shape of the block needed to cover the pictured shape in Exercise **A**. With the students still working in pairs, ask one student in each pair to find a block with the correct attribute and place it on the picture. Then ask the other student in each pair to complete the exercise by choosing a sufficient number of blocks with the same shape and placing each block in a dotted circle. Work with the students to complete Exercise **B**; then distribute Activity Sheet 170. Allow students to work simultaneously on the two exercises to complete the activity.

Grouping by Shape or Color (Activity 171–172)

Objectives:
Using INTERLOCKING CUBES:
1. construct figures to match pictures
2. classify figures according to color and shape

Materials:
For each group of six students • One set of INTERLOCKING CUBES

For each student   • Activity Sheets 171–172
                                                    • Crayons

Teacher Instructions:
This lesson is last in a series that explores the task of classifying objects using the attributes of shape and color and constructing a set based on these attributes. The INTERLOCKING CUBES enable the concept to be extended to more complex figures. Continue encouraging discussion based upon the attributes of the figures and emphasizing the attributes or properties of the entire set of figures rather than a comparison of individual pieces within the set, e.g., "*All* the figures in the set are the same shape," or "Each set has a different color of figures."

Classroom Activity:
Ask each student to select four sets of four cubes from the set of INTERLOCK-ING CUBES with each set a different color. Hold up a **T-shaped figure** made of four cubes and ask the students to construct two matching figures with two of their four sets. Hold up an **L-shaped figure** made of four cubes and ask the students to construct two matching figures with their remaining sets of cubes. After they complete the construction task, have students compare figures to determine whether all students have figures with the same color and shape. Ask the students to group figures with the same shape to make sets. (The sets should contain figures of different colors.) Encourage students to compare sets and use the attributes of shape and color to verbalize the differences they find.

Distribute Activity Sheet 171 and, working with pairs of students, ask each pair to select two sets of ten cubes from the set of INTERLOCKING CUBES; each set should be a different color. Allow time for each pair of students to construct the figures at the top of the sheet (two of each figure). Ask one student in each pair to place the correct figure on the picture in Exercise **A** on the second student's sheet. Discuss with the students the figures that have the attributes necessary to complete the exercise (same shape, ignore color). The second student in the pair should then locate the figures to place in the box (same shape) and complete the exercise. Reverse the students' roles and repeat the task by locating the figures needed to complete Exercise **B** on the other student's sheet. Allow students to work in pairs to complete the remaining exercise on their sheets, then continue with Activity Sheet 172, stressing that the exercises on this sheet involve the attribute of color.

Grouping by Color (Activity 173–174)

Objectives:
> Using ATTRIBUTE BLOCKS:
> 1. match blocks with pictures of shapes
> 2. classify sets of blocks according to color

Materials:
> For each group of six students • One set of ATTRIBUTE BLOCKS
>
> For each student   • Activity Sheets 173–174
>   • Crayons

Teacher Instructions:
> This lesson is the first in a series using ATTRIBUTE BLOCKS to classify blocks according to one or more attributes. The initial activity involves students in building a set of blocks based upon the attribute of color. The Activity Sheets require students to construct a set of blocks with the same color but different shapes and include pictures of the shapes to be selected for the construction. Later lessons will eliminate this perceptual cue. Continue encouraging the students to verbalize the attributes of the entire sets of blocks.

Classroom Activity:
> Separate the ATTRIBUTE BLOCKS into large and small shapes, return the small blocks to their containers, and ask each group of six to sort the blocks by thickness. One group of three will use the fifteen thin blocks and the other will use the fifteen thick blocks. Hold up a **large red triangle-shape,** asking one student in each group to find a block with the same shape and same color. Next, ask a second student in each group to find a block with the same color but a different shape. The third student in each group should then find another block with the same color but a third shape. After the students return all the blocks to the set, hold up a **large blue hexagon-shape.** Ask each group of three to make a set of blocks that includes all the shapes that have the same color. Discuss the attributes of the sets they have created with the students (same color, different shapes and thicknesses). Repeat the activity with different colors and blocks as time permits.
>
> Remove the small blocks from their containers and return the large blocks to their proper locations. Distribute Activity Sheets 173 and 174 and ask one student to find the matching block of the correct color to cover the top shape in Exercise **A** on Sheet 173. Ask another student to find a block with the same color and cover another shape in the box on the same sheet. Continue until all the pictured shapes have been covered with blocks of the same color. Since both thick and thin blocks are needed to complete the task, stress that this attribute can be ignored when selecting the blocks. After students complete this activity, have them work in pairs to complete the two sheets. Remind them to select blocks of the same color to cover the pictured shapes in each exercise and to color the pictures to match the blocks. Pairs will need to share and exchange blocks to complete the exercises.

Grouping—Color and Shape (Activity 175–176)

Objectives:
> Using ATTRIBUTE BLOCKS:
> 1. match blocks with pictures of shapes
> 2. classify sets of blocks according to color and shape

Materials:
> For each group of six students • One set of ATTRIBUTE BLOCKS
>
> For each student   • Activity Sheets 175–176
>   • Crayons

Teacher Instructions:
> This lesson continues developing the concept of classifying ATTRIBUTE BLOCKS according to one or more attributes. The initial activities and the Activity Sheets both involve the task of building a set of blocks based upon the properties of same shape and same color. Perceptual cues, provided in earlier lessons by including pictures of the shapes necessary to construct each set, have been eliminated. Continue encouraging the students to verbalize those attributes that are the same and those that are different for each set of blocks.

Classroom Activity:
> After separating the ATTRIBUTE BLOCKS into large and small shapes, return the small blocks to their containers and ask each group of six students to sort the large blocks by color. Each pair of students should then select a set of the sorted blocks. Hold up a **large red circle-shape** and ask each pair to determine whether they have blocks that are the same color. Each student in the pair with the matching color blocks should then select a block that matches the circle-shape and show it to the other students. Discuss the fact that other students have the same shapes, but they are a different color. Hold up a **large yellow square-shape** and alter the procedure by first asking students to find the matching shape, then determining which pair has the matching color. Repeat the activity with blocks of various shapes and colors as time permits.
>
> Remove the small blocks from their containers and return the large blocks to their proper locations. After distributing Activity Sheets 175 and 176, ask one student in each group to find a block with the correct color and shape to cover the picture in Exercise **A** on Sheet 175. Discuss with the students other blocks that could be placed in the box. (The blocks should have the same shape and same color.) Since both thick and thin blocks are needed to complete the task, stress that this attribute can be ignored when selecting blocks to place in the box. Ask a second student in each group to choose the appropriate block to complete the exercise, place it in the box, trace the block, and color the picture. After this exercise is finished, students should work in pairs on different exercises on both sheets, using the attributes of shape and color to construct each set of blocks.

Grouping—Color and Shape (Activity 177–178)

Objectives:
Using ATTRIBUTE BLOCKS:
1. match blocks with pictures of shapes
2. classify sets of blocks according to color and shape

Materials:
For each group of six students • One set of ATTRIBUTE BLOCKS

For each student   • Activity Sheets 177–178
                                                  • Crayons

Teacher Instructions:
This lesson extends the concept of classifying ATTRIBUTE BLOCKS according to one or more attributes by requiring students to generalize to blocks that are the same shape but a different color. Begin encouraging the students to change the focus of their attention from comparing individual blocks to using the attributes of shape and color when verbalizing the criteria for a specific set, e.g., *all* the blocks in the set are the same shape, but they are different colors.

Classroom Activity:
Separate the ATTRIBUTE BLOCKS by size, return the small blocks to their containers, and ask each group of six students to sort the large blocks by color. Each pair of students should then select a single set of blocks. Hold up a **large yellow triangle-shape** and ask each pair to determine whether their blocks are the same color. Each student in the pair with the yellow blocks should then select a block that matches the triangle-shape and show it to the other students. Other pairs of students should then select blocks that have the same shape but a different color, construct a new set with the selected blocks, and describe the comparative attributes of their sets and the triangle-shape (same shape and size, different color). Then focus the discussion on comparing the three sets constructed within the group. Hold up another block and repeat the procedure.

Remove the small blocks from their containers and return the large blocks to their proper locations. With students working in groups of three, ask them to separate the blocks by thickness, providing fifteen blocks for each group. Distribute Activity Sheets 177 and 178, then ask one student in each group to find a block that should be used to cover the pictured shape in Exercise **A** on Sheet 177. Help the students determine which other blocks should be placed in the box. (The blocks should be the same shape but a different color.) Next, ask each of the other two students in each group to select a block, place it in the box, trace the block, and color the pictures to complete the exercise. Rotate the tasks among the three students until the exercise is completed on each student's Activity Sheet. Allow students to continue working in groups of three on different exercises to finish the two sheets. Assist students with the constructions, encouraging them to use the attributes of shape and color when describing their choices.

Grouping—Color and Shape (Activity 179–180)

Objectives:
> Using ATTRIBUTE BLOCKS:
> 1. match blocks with pictures of shapes
> 2. classify sets of blocks according to color and shape

Materials:
> For each group of six students • One set of ATTRIBUTE BLOCKS
>
> For each student   • Activity Sheets 179–180
>   • Crayons

Teacher Instructions:
> This lesson continues to help students explore the concept of classifying ATTRIBUTE BLOCKS according to one or more attributes. The activities require that students construct sets of blocks that have the same color as a given block but a different shape. Continue encouraging the students to describe the criteria for a complete set, focusing on the attributes of shape and color, rather than comparing individual blocks. Since the box in each Activity Sheet exercise is not large enough to hold all the blocks that satisfy the properties of the set, the constructed sets will differ from student to student.

Classroom Activity:
> After separating the ATTRIBUTE BLOCKS into large and small shapes, return the small blocks to their containers. Ask each group of six students to sort the large blocks by thickness to provide each group of three with a set of fifteen blocks. Hold up a **large blue hexagon-shape** and ask each group to locate a matching block in their set. Then ask the students to find other blocks with the same color but a different shape than the hexagon-shape. After each student has selected a block, encourage them to compare their blocks verbally to your hexagon-shape using the attributes of shape and color. Have the students select the remaining blocks that satisfy the conditions of same color/different shape and construct a set. Encourage them to compare the newly constructed set of blocks to your block. (All the blocks are the same color but a different shape.) Repeat the procedure with a **large red rectangle-shape**.
>
> Remove the small blocks from their containers and return the large blocks to their proper locations. Ask the students to separate the blocks by thickness so that each group of three has fifteen blocks. After distributing Activity Sheets 179 and 180, ask one student in each group to find the block to cover the shape pictured in Exercise **A** on Sheet 179. Work with the students to determine which other blocks should be placed in the box (same color, different shape) and have each of the other students in the group select a block that belongs in the box. The three students should then find the remaining blocks that satisfy the conditions of same color/different shape, complete the construction, trace the blocks, and color the pictures. Have the two groups of students rotate the tasks as they work on different exercises to complete the two sheets.

Grouping—Color and Shape (Activity 181–182)

Objectives:
>   Using ATTRIBUTE BLOCKS:
>   1. match blocks with pictures of shapes
>   2. classify sets of blocks according to color and shape

Materials:
>   For each group of six students   • One set of ATTRIBUTE BLOCKS
>
>   For each student   • Activity Sheets 181–182
>   • Crayons

Teacher Instructions:
>   This activity continues the task of classifying shapes by more than one attribute and requires students to construct a set of ATTRIBUTE BLOCKS that differs from a given block by both shape and color. Continue to focus on the criteria for set membership rather than restricting discussion to comparing individual blocks. The box in each Activity Sheet exercise is not large enough to hold all the blocks that satisfy the properties of the set, so the constructed sets will again differ from student to student.

Classroom Activity:
>   After separating the ATTRIBUTE BLOCKS by size, return the small blocks to their containers. Ask each group of six to sort the large blocks by color and each pair within the group to select a set of a single color. Hold up a **large yellow circle-shape** and ask each pair to construct a set of all their blocks that are *not* circle-shapes. Discuss with the students the fact that one pair of students has a set that is not circle-shapes but does have the same color as the block you are holding, while the other pairs of students have sets of blocks that differ by both shape and color. Repeat the procedure with a **large red hexagon-shape**, asking students to compare their sets verbally to the original block.

>   Remove the small blocks from their containers and return the large blocks to their proper locations. Ask the students to sort the blocks by thickness so that each group of three has fifteen blocks. After distributing Activity Sheets 181 and 182, ask one student in each group to find a block that matches the shape pictured in Exercise **A** on Sheet 181. Work with the students to determine which of the remaining blocks could be placed in the set (different color and shape). Then ask the other two students in each group to select a block that belongs in the box. The three students should then find the remaining blocks that satisfy the conditions of different color and shape, and complete the construction by placing four or five blocks within the box. Stress that not all the blocks in the set will fit into the box. Have two groups of three work on different exercises on the two sheets, rotating the tasks until all the activities are complete.

Describing a Group—What Does Not Belong? (Activity 183–184)

Objectives:
Using ATTRIBUTE BLOCKS:
1. define a set by the property of color
2. remove shapes that are not members of a set

Materials:
For each group of six students • One set of ATTRIBUTE BLOCKS .

For each student   • Activity Sheets 183–184
                                       • Crayons

Teacher Instructions:
This lesson uses ATTRIBUTE BLOCKS to introduce a series of activities designed to develop the ability of defining a set of objects using one or more attributes. These activities present the task of describing sets based on the attributes of color and/or thickness. Encourage the students to look for attributes that are common to all blocks within a set rather than restricting their description to a comparison of individual pairs of blocks. This perspective is especially necessary for the more suble task of looking for attributes shared by the majority of the blocks within a given group.

Classroom Activity:
Remove the large ATTRIBUTE BLOCKS from their containers and ask each group of students to separate the blocks by thickness. The students should then sort the resulting two sets by color to create one set for each student. Discuss the property common to all the blocks in their individual sets with the students. (All the blocks are the same color.) Hold up a **large thick blue triangle-shape** and ask the students to compare it to the blocks in their sets. Determine which student has a set of blocks with the same color and thickness as your triangle-shape, then encourage the other students to explain why the block does not belong in their sets (wrong color and/or thickness). Repeat the task using other blocks and continue asking the students to verbalize why particular blocks do or do not not belong to their sets.

Remove the small blocks from their containers and return the large blocks to their proper locations. Distribute Activity Sheet 183 and work with the students to select blocks with the correct color and shape to cover the pictures in Exercise **A** (ignore thick/thin attribute). Ask each student to place a block on the set on one student's sheet . Discuss the attributes of the group of blocks used to cover the picture, focusing the discussion on the fact that all the blocks except one are the same color. Ask one student to remove the block that is a different color and encourage the students to verbalize the property of the remaining set of blocks (all the same color). Distribute Activity Sheet 184 and allow students to continue working in pairs on different exercises to complete the two sheets. Have them cover the pictures, remove the block that does not belong, and color the pictures of those shapes with the common attribute of color.

Describing a Group—What Does Not Belong? (Activity 185–186)

Objectives:
Using ATTRIBUTE BLOCKS:
1. define a set by the property of shape
2. remove blocks that are not members of a set

Materials:
For each group of six students • One set of ATTRIBUTE BLOCKS

For each student   • Activity Sheets 185-186
                                                    • Crayons

Teacher Instructions:
This lesson uses ATTRIBUTE BLOCKS to continue developing the ability to define a set of objects using one or more attributes. These activities present the task of describing sets based upon the attributes of shape and/or thickness. Continue encouraging the students to look for attributes common to all blocks within a set, rather than restricting their comparison to individual pairs of blocks. This extended perspective is necessary for the more subtle task of looking for those attributes common to the majority of the blocks within a given group.

Classroom Activity:
Remove the large ATTRIBUTE BLOCKS from their containers and ask each group of six to separate their blocks by shape. With the students working in pairs, ask them to select one of the following block sets: **circle-shapes**, **rectangle-shapes**, or **hexagon-shapes**. Discuss with the students the property common to all the blocks in their individual sets. (All the blocks are the same shape.) Hold up a **large circle-shape** and ask the students to compare it to the blocks in their sets. After determining which students have a set of circle-shaped blocks, encourage the other pairs to explain why your block does not belong in their sets (wrong shape). Repeat the task with other shapes, and continue asking students to explain why each block does or does not belong to their sets.

Remove the small blocks from their containers and return the large blocks to their proper locations. Distribute Activity Sheet 185 and work with the students to select blocks with the correct color and shape (ignore thickness) to cover the pictures in Exercise **A**. Each student should then cover one picture in Exercise **A** on one student's Activity Sheet. Discuss with the students the attributes of the group of blocks used to cover the pictures, focusing on the fact that all blocks except one are the same shape. Ask one student to remove the block that is different, and encourage the students to verbalize the property of the resulting set. (All the blocks are the same shape.) Allow time for students to color the shapes, then distribute Activity Sheet 186. Have students work in pairs on the remaining exercises to cover the pictures, remove the block that does not belong, and color the pictures that have the attribute of shape in common.

Describing a Group—What Does Not Belong? (Activity 187-188)

Objectives:
  Using PATTERN BLOCKS:
    1. define a set by the properties of shape and/or color
    2. remove blocks that are not members of a set

Materials:
  For each group of six students • One set of PATTERN BLOCKS

  For each student   • Activity Sheets 187–188
             • Crayons

Teacher Instructions:
  Using PATTERN BLOCKS, this lesson continues to explore the concept of employing one or more attributes to define a set of objects. These activities present sets based upon the attribute of shape, but, since PATTERN BLOCK shapes are color-coded, students may use shape and/orcolor to define criteria for set membership. Continue to encourage the students to look for attributes shared by all blocks within a set, rather than restricting their comparison to individual pairs of blocks. This extended perspective is necessary for the more subtle task of looking for attributes common to the majority of blocks within a given group.

Classroom Activity:
  Ask each student in the group to select a different shape and construct a matching set of five blocks from the PATTERN BLOCK set. Discuss with the students the properties common to all the blocks in each individual set. (All are the same shape and color.) Hold up a **trapezoid** (red) and ask the students to compare it with their sets to determine which students have sets with the same shape and color as the trapezoid. Encourage the other students to explain why the block does not belong to their sets (wrong shape and/or color). Repeat the task with other blocks, encouraging students to explain why each block does or does not belong to their set.

  After distributing Activity Sheet 187, work with the students to choose blocks that match the shapes pictured in Exercise **A**. With students working in pairs, ask them to cover the pictures on one student's paper. Discuss the attributes of the group of blocks used to cover the pictures, focusing on the fact that all the blocks except one are the same shape and color. Ask one student in each pair to remove the block that is different, and encourage students to verbalize the property of the resulting set. (All the blocks have the same shape and same color.) Distribute Activity Sheet 188 and have the students continue to work in pairs on the remaining exercises. They should select the blocks, cover the shapes, remove the block that does not belong, and color the pictures that have the attribute of shape in common.

Describing a Group—Adding Shapes (Activity 189–190)

Objectives:
Using PATTERN BLOCKS:
1. define a set by the properties of shape and/or color
2. add blocks that can belong to the set

Materials:
For each group of six students   • One set of PATTERN BLOCKS

For each student   • Activity Sheets 189–190
                                        • Crayons

Teacher Instructions:
This lesson introduces a series of activities using PATTERN BLOCKS for further exploration in defining a set of objects using one or more attributes. While earlier lessons focused on identifying blocks that were not members of a given set, this lesson begins the process of adding blocks to a given set and reinforces the concept of describing sets based upon the attributes of shape and/or color. Since the blocks are color-coded, students may continue to use shape, color, or both to define criteria for a set. Encourage the students to look for attributes shared by all blocks within a set, rather than restricting their description to a comparison of individual pairs of blocks.

Classroom Activity:
Ask each student to select two different shapes and construct two sets of five matching blocks from the set of PATTERN BLOCKS. Discuss with the students the properties common to all the blocks in each of their sets. (All blocks within each set are the same shape and color.) Hold up a **square** (orange), ask the students to compare it with their sets, and determine which students could add the block to one of their sets. Encourage students to verbalize *why* the square could be added to one of their sets but not the other. Repeat the task with other blocks as time permits.

Distribute Activity Sheet 189 and work with the students to select blocks to cover the shapes pictured in Exercise **A**. With students working in pairs, ask them to cover the pictures on one student's paper. Discuss the attributes of the blocks they used to cover the pictures, and focus the students' attention on the fact that all the blocks are the same shape and color. Ask one student in each pair to select a block that could be added to the set in Exercise **A**, encouraging the students to verbalize that the new set has the same attributes as the original set; i.e., all the blocks still have the same shape and color. Allow time for the tracing and coloring activity, then distribute Activity Sheet 190 and have students continue working in pairs to complete the two sheets. They should choose the necessary blocks, cover the pictured shapes, add another block (or blocks) to each set, then trace the blocks and color the pictures.

Describing a Group—Adding Shapes (Activity 191–192)

Objectives:
Using ATTRIBUTE BLOCKS:
1. define a set by the property of color
2. add blocks that can belong to the set

Materials:
For each group of six students • One set of ATTRIBUTE BLOCKS

For each student   • Activity Sheets 191–192
                                • Crayons

Teacher Instructions:
This lesson uses ATTRIBUTE BLOCKS to continue exploring the concept of defining a set of objects by one or more attributes. While earlier lessons focused on identifying blocks that were *not* members of a given set, this lesson focuses on adding blocks to a given set. Introductory activities ask students to describe sets based upon the attributes of color and/or thickness. Continue to stress that the students should consider attributes shared by *all* blocks within a set, rather than restricting their description to individual pairs of blocks.

Classroom Activity:
Remove the large ATTRIBUTE BLOCKS from their containers and ask each group of students to sort their blocks first by thickness, then by color, creating one set for each student. Help the students determine the property common to all the blocks in their individual sets. (All blocks have the same color and thickness.) Hold up a **large thick red hexagon-shape** and ask the students to compare it to the blocks in their sets. After they determine who has a set with blocks the same color and thickness as the hexagon-shape, allow that student to add the block to his/her set, and encourage the other students to explain why the block cannot be added to their sets (wrong color and/or wrong thickness). Repeat the task until one block has been added to each student's set.

Remove the small blocks from their containers and return the large blocks to their proper locations. Distribute Activity Sheet 191 and work with the students to select blocks with the correct color and shape (ignore thickness) to cover the pictures in Exercise **A**. Discuss blocks that could be added to the set (four choices), and allow students to select the block they wish, place it in the box, then trace the block and color the pictures. Repeat the procedure, constructing a set of blocks to cover the pictures in Exercise **B**, then choosing and adding other blocks to the sets. Again, discuss the common attribute of the set. Distribute Activity Sheet 192 and allow students to work individually to complete the exercises. The block selected to complete each exercise should vary from student to student, and they will need to share and exchange blocks to complete the exercises on the two sheets.

Describing a Group—Adding Shapes (Activity 193–194)

Objectives:
>Using ATTRIBUTE BLOCKS:
>1. define a set by the property of shape
>2. add blocks that can belong to a set

Materials:
>For each group of six students • One set of ATTRIBUTE BLOCKS

>For each student   • Activity Sheets 193–194
>   • Crayons

Teacher Instructions:
>This lesson continues using ATTRIBUTE BLOCKS to explore the concept of defining a set by one or more attributes, then adding blocks to that set. Introductory activities include the task of describing sets based upon the attributes of shape and color. Continue stressing to students that they are looking for attributes shared by *all* blocks within a set, not comparing individual blocks.

Classroom Activity:
>Working with the large ATTRIBUTE BLOCKS, ask each group to separate their blocks by shape; then ask each pair in the group to select one block set: **circle-shapes**, **triangle-shapes**, or **hexagon-shapes**. Discuss with the students the property common to all blocks in their individual sets. (All blocks are the same shape.) Hold up a **large circle-shape** and ask the students to compare it to their sets to determine which pair has a matching set of blocks (circle-shapes). Allow those students to add your block to their set, and encourage the other students to explain why the block cannot be added to their sets (wrong shape). Repeat the activity until two blocks have been added to each pair's set.

>Remove the small blocks from their containers and return the large blocks to their proper locations. Distribute Activity Sheet 193 and work with the students to select the correct blocks to cover the shapes pictured in Exercise **A** (ignore thickness). Stress the common attribute of the set (same shape), then discuss which blocks could be added to the set (two choices). Allow time for students to select the appropriate blocks, trace them in the box, and color the pictures. Repeat the procedure, helping the students construct a set to cover the pictures in Exercise **B**, add the chosen block to the set, trace it, and color the pictures to match the blocks. Distribute Activity Sheet 194, pointing out to the students that two blocks must be added to each exercise on the page. Allow students to work individually to complete the exercises, but remind them that they will need to share and exchange blocks to complete the exercises.

Describing a Group—What Belongs? (Activity 195–196)

Objectives:
Using ATTRIBUTE BLOCKS:
1. select blocks to match pictures
2. assign blocks to a set based upon one attribute

Materials:
For each group of six students • One set of ATTRIBUTE BLOCKS

For each student   • Activity Sheets 195–196
                                                  • A pencil or crayons

Teacher Instructions:
This lesson continues using ATTRIBUTE BLOCKS to develop the ability of defining set properties and using the definition to assign additional blocks to the set. Initial activities include placing large blocks into a similar set of small blocks. This emphasizes that only shape or color are relevant attributes in each exercise and that size can be disregarded. If this creates confusion, restrict the activity to blocks of the same size. Since the sets of shapes pictured on the Activity Sheets are smaller than the actual blocks, students will be unable to verify their answers by placing each block directly on the picture. If they encounter difficulty with these tasks, permit them to use the blocks to copy the pictured sets of shapes.

Classroom Activity:
Using the small ATTRIBUTE BLOCKS, ask each group of six to sort the blocks by thickness. One group of three should then sort the thick blocks by color, providing each with a complete color set, while the other group of three sorts the thin blocks by shape, selecting the following shape sets: triangle, hexagon, and square. Hold up two **large red square-shapes**, ask students to describe their individual sets, then determine whether either block could be placed in their set. Discuss with the students that the attribute of size can be ignored, and focus on the attributes of shape and color. Encourage students to explain why each block will or will not fit in their sets. After placing your blocks in the appropriate sets by color and shape, repeat the activity with other blocks until one block has been placed in each student's set.

Regroup the individual sets, forming one set of thick blocks and one set of thin blocks for each group of six. Distribute Activity Sheets 195 and 196. With each group of three working with either a thick or thin block set, ask various students to place blocks on the shapes pictured in the first column on one student's copy of Sheet 195. Discuss the properties of the first group of shapes (same shape), and help the students decide which block from the column could be added to that group. Repeat the process for the remaining groups and shapes on the page. Allow students to continue working in groups of three, rotating the tasks of covering pictures and drawing a line to connect the blocks with the correct groups.

Describing a Group—What Belongs? (Activity 197–198)

Objectives:
Using INTERLOCKING CUBES:
1. construct figures to match pictures
2. assign figures to sets based on one attribute

Materials:
For each group of six students • One set of INTERLOCKING CUBES

For each student   • Activity Sheets 197–198
                                    • A pencil or crayons

Teacher Instructions:
This lesson uses INTERLOCKING CUBES to further develop the ability to define a set and assign additional figures to the set based upon that definition. Since the sets of figures pictured on the Activity Sheets are smaller than the actual cubes, students will be unable to verify their answers by placing each figure on the pictures. If they encounter difficulty with these tasks, permit them to construct the cube figures pictured in each group. Placing the groups on the right portion of the page instead of the left portion also introduces a subtle complication. It is easier for students to first define a group, then find a figure that belongs to it, rather than beginning with a figure, then trying to place it in the correct group. Students will, therefore, find it easier to work from the right column to the left column to complete the exercises.

Classroom Activity:
Using INTERLOCKING CUBES, ask each student to make five sets of four matching cubes, with each set a different color. Each student should then use these sets to construct **three lengths of four cubes** and **two L-shaped figures**. Ask them to place the figures into a combined set, then ask various students to create the following sets: three red figures of different shapes; three yellow figures of different shapes; three L-shaped figures of different colors; and three lengths of four different colored cubes. (Two sets are based on color, and two on shape.) Ask one student to select a figure from the remaining group and determine in which two sets it could be placed, based on color or shape. Repeat the process with other students until all remaining figures have been assigned to a set.

Distribute Activity Sheet 197 and allow students to work in pairs to construct the figures and cover the pictures in the left column on one student's sheet. Help the students determine the properties of the first group of figures on the page, encouraging them to describe the groups in terms of shape and/or color. After they decide which figure can belong in the first group, repeat the procedure with the remaining groups of figures. Distribute Activity Sheet 198 and allow students to continue working in pairs to complete the two sheets: constructing the figures, covering the pictures, and drawing a line connecting the picture of each figure to the appropriate group. Note that Figure **4** can be placed in either the first or second group (group one by shape and group two by color). Emphasize that *each* figure must be placed and that *each* group must be used.

Separating Groups by Color (Activity 199–200)

Objectives:
Using ATTRIBUTE BLOCKS:
1. match blocks with pictures
2. assign blocks to a set based on one attribute

Materials:
For each group of six students • One set of ATTRIBUTE BLOCKS

For each student
• Activity Sheets 199–200
• Crayons

Teacher Instructions:
This lesson begins a series of activities using ATTRIBUTE BLOCKS to explore the concept of separating groups based on a single attribute while ignoring other attributes. In this lesson, both the initial activity and the Activity Sheets focus on the attribute of color. The initial activity presents sets of blocks that differ by shape and size, while the Activity Sheets include the variables of shape and thickness. Later lessons will introduce sets that have the common attribute of size, shape, or number of sides.

Classroom Activity:
Separate a set of ATTRIBUTE BLOCKS by thickness, providing each group of three with a set of thirty thick or thin blocks. Ask each student in the group to choose a specific color and collect all the blocks of that color. (Each student should have ten blocks.) Discuss the attributes of their individual sets with the students, emphasizing that although each set contains blocks of varying shapes and sizes, it has a common attribute of color. Reassemble the blocks to again form one set of thick and one set of thin shapes, and continue the activity, rotating the color assignments among the students, until each has collected a set of shapes in each color. Continue encouraging students to verbalize the common attribute of each set they construct.

Return the large blocks to the container, then distribute Activity Sheet 199. With students working in groups of three, ask them to select a set of blocks that could be used to cover the pictures at the top of the page. Encourage each group to use both thick and thin blocks in constructing their set. Discuss the properties of the set with the students. (The blocks are all the same size, but of different shapes, thicknesses, and colors.) Ask two students in each group to place the blocks on the third student's sheet. That student should then move the blocks to the appropriate boxes at the bottom of the page using the attribute of color. Again, ask the students to verbalize the common attribute of each individual set formed by the separation and to compare and contrast the two resulting sets. Distribute Activity Sheet 200 and allow students to continue working in groups, rotating tasks among students and allowing time for the tracing and coloring activities, until all sheets are complete.

Separating Groups by Shape (Activity 201–202)

Objectives:

Using ATTRIBUTE BLOCKS:
1. match blocks with pictures
2. assign blocks to a set based on a single attribute

Materials:

For each group of six students • One set of ATTRIBUTE BLOCKS

For each student   • Activity Sheets 201–202
                                • Crayons

Teacher Instructions:

This lesson continues to use ATTRIBUTE BLOCKS in exploring the concept of separating groups based on a single attribute while ignoring the remaining attributes. Both the initial activity and Activity Sheets for this lesson focus on the attribute of shape. The initial activity presents sets of blocks that differ by color and size, while the Activity Sheets include the variables of color and thickness. Later lessons will focus on separating groups by the attributes of size or number of sides.

Classroom Activity:

Separate a set of large and small ATTRIBUTE BLOCKS by thickness to provide each group of three students with a set of thirty blocks. Assign each student a specific shape and ask him/her to collect all the blocks with that shape. (Each student should have six blocks, three large and three small.) Discuss the attributes of their individual sets of blocks with the students, emphasizing that although each set contains blocks of various colors and sizes, each has the attribute of shape in common. Reassemble the sets of thick and thin blocks and continue the activity, assigning students different shapes until each has collected a set of the five different shapes. Continue to encourage students to verbalize the common attribute of each set they construct.

Return the large blocks to the container, then distribute Activity Sheet 201. With students working in groups of three, ask them to form a set of thick and thin blocks that could be used to cover the pictures at the top of the page. Discuss the properties of the set with the students. (The blocks are all the same size, but differ in shape, thickness, and color.) Request two students in each group to place the chosen blocks on the third student's sheet. That student should then move the blocks into the appropriate box at the bottom of the page according to the attribute of shape. Ask the students to verbalize the common attributes of each individual set formed by the separation and to compare and contrast the resulting two sets. After distributing Activity Sheet 202, allow students to continue to work in groups, rotating tasks among students and allowing time for the tracing and coloring activity, until all sheets are complete.

Separating Groups by Shape (Activity 203–204)

Objectives:
Using PATTERN BLOCKS:
1. match blocks with pictures
2. assign blocks to a set based on a single attribute

Materials:
For each group of six students • One set of PATTERN BLOCKS

For each student   • Activity Sheets 203–204
                                • Crayons

Teacher Instructions:
This lesson continues to use PATTERN BLOCKS to explore of the task of separating groups of blocks according to a single attribute while ignoring the remaining attributes. The attribute of shape is used to define a set of blocks in the initial activities, which also introduces the idea of counting the number of sides as a basis for grouping. This attribute will be used in the next lesson as the basis for separating the blocks into two sets. The Activity Sheets in this lesson focus on the attribute of shape.

Classroom Activity:
Ask students in each group of six to construct the following block sets: one pair should select six **tan rhombuses**; a second pair should select six **trapezoids** (red); one student should select six **blue rhombuses**; and the last student should select six **squares** (orange). Ask the students to combine their sets as follows: **squares–tan rhombuses, trapezoids–blue rhombuses**, and **tan rhombuses–trapezoids**. Discuss the properties of the newly-formed sets with the students. (The blocks in each set have different shapes and colors, but the same number of sides.) Encourage students to verbalize differences between the blocks within each set, but stress that they have the attribute "number of sides" in common. Ask the students to separate their groups of sets by shape until each student has his/her original set again. Repeat the task as time permits, making sets with other block combinations and discussing their comparative attributes.

Distribute Activity Sheets 203 and 204. With the students working in pairs, ask them to construct the set of blocks to cover the shapes pictured at the top of Sheet 203. Discuss the properties of the set (different colors and shapes, but same number of sides). Repeat the selection task for the second page, again discussing the set's attributes (different colors and shapes). Each student should then place a set of blocks on the pictures on one sheet, place each block in the appropriate box at the bottom of the page, trace the blocks, and color the pictures. Rotate the block sets between each pair of students as they complete the exercises on the two sheets.

Separating Groups by Shape (Activity 205–206)

Objectives:
Using PATTERN BLOCKS:
1. construct a set to match a picture of shapes
2. assign blocks to a set based on a single attribute

Materials:
For each group of six students • One set of PATTERN BLOCKS

For each student   • Activity Sheets 205–206
                                         • Crayons

Teacher Instructions:
This lesson continues to employ PATTERN BLOCKS in developing the skill of separating a group of blocks according to a single attribute while ignoring the remaining attributes. The initial activities require the students to separate the set of blocks using the attribute "number of sides." Students may have difficulty seeing that hexagons and triangles may belong in the same set, since they have a different number of sides. Stress that the attribute being used to sort the blocks is "four sides" versus "not four sides."

Classroom Activity:
Divide each set of PATTERN BLOCKS into three sets, with each containing approximately the same number of blocks and all six shapes. With the students working in pairs, ask one of each pair to remove all the blocks with four sides from the set of blocks and the other student to make a set containing all the blocks that *do not* have four sides. Discuss the properties of the newly formed sets with the students. Emphasize that the set constructed by one student in each pair has blocks with different colors and shapes, but the same number of sides, while the other set contains blocks that differ by shape, color, *and* number of sides. If time permits, repeat the activity using three sides or six sides as the grouping attribute.

Distribute Activity Sheets 205 and 206. Working with students in pairs, ask each pair to construct a set of blocks to cover the pictures at the top of Sheet 205. Discuss the properties of the set (different colors, shapes, and number of sides) with the students. Repeat the task and discussion of attributes (different colors, shapes, and number of sides) for the second sheet. Stress that some blocks in the set at the top of the second sheet have different colors and shapes, but the same number of sides. Have each student place a set of blocks on the pictures on one sheet, separate the blocks into the appropriate box on the bottom of the sheet, trace the blocks, and color the pictures. Rotate the block sets between students so that each can complete the exercises on the two sheets.

Separating Groups by Size (Activity 207–208)

Objectives:
Using INTERLOCKING CUBES:
1. construct figures to match pictures
2. assign figures to sets based on a single attribute

Materials:
For each group of six students • One set of INTERLOCKING CUBES

For each student   • Activity Sheets 207–208
                                                 • Crayons

Teacher Instructions:
This is the last in a series of activities focusing on the ability to separate a group of figures according to a single attribute while ignoring the remaining attributes. The lesson also extends the previous activity of counting the number of sides of a block to that of counting the number of cubes. Although students may sort the figures by shape, encourage them to count the cubes used in constructing the various figures. Both the initial activities and the Activity Sheets are intended to emphasize separating the sets of INTERLOCKING CUBE figures according to this attribute. When they are constructing the figures needed for the Activity Sheets, encourage the students to vary the color of the cubes from figure to figure so that color will not become a misleading cue.

Classroom Activity:
With the students working in pairs, ask one in each pair to make four sets of three cubes using four different colors and the other student to use the same four colors to make four sets of four cubes. (All the cubes in each set should be the same color.) The first student should use his/her four sets to construct **two lengths of three cubes** and **two L-shaped figures** with the remaining six cubes, while the second student constructs **two lengths of four cubes** and **two L-shaped figures** with the remaining eight cubes. Ask each pair to place their figures into a single set and discuss how the combined set of figures could be sorted (color, shape, number of cubes). Have each student choose a set from the figures constructed by the other student. Discuss with students the common attribute of their selected sets of figures.

Distribute Activity Sheet 207 and allow individual students time to construct the figures and cover the pictures at the top of the sheet. After students place the figures on the pictures, discuss the attributes of the figures within the group with the students. (They have different colors, shapes, and number of cubes.) Encourage the students to describe the figures by comparing the number of cubes. After the students decide which figures should be placed in each bottom box, allow them time to separate the groups, trace the figures, and color the pictures. Distribute Activity Sheet 208 and have the students repeat the tasks: constructing the figures, covering the pictures, separating the group, then tracing the figures and coloring the pictures to match the cubes.

Forming a Group—Shape and Color (Activity 209–210)

Objectives:
Using ATTRIBUTE BLOCKS:
1. classify blocks by a single attribute
2. construct a set of blocks that satisfies two attributes

Materials:
For each group of six students • One set of ATTRIBUTE BLOCKS

For each student   • Activity Sheets 209–210
                                                 • Crayons

Teacher Instructions:
This lesson uses ATTRIBUTE BLOCKS to introduce the task of constructing a set that has two common attributes. The activity introduces consideration of another characteristic of ATTRIBUTE BLOCKS: the number of sides of a block. This attribute is used as a basis for two complementary tasks: constructing a set that contains blocks with the same number of sides, and constructing a set that contains blocks with a different numbers of sides. Thus, although squares and rectangles are different shapes, both have four sides and, consequently, the set constructed on Activity Sheet 209 will contain both blocks. This factor will become more important in later lessons using PATTERN BLOCKS, since four different blocks have the same number of sides.

Classroom Activity:
Separate the ATTRIBUTE BLOCKS into large and small shapes, return the small blocks to their containers, and ask each group of six students to sort the large blocks by thickness. One group of three students will use the fifteen thick blocks while the other uses the fifteen thin blocks. Hold up a **large red triangle-shape** and ask one student in each group to locate all the blocks that have the same number of sides and the same color as your block. Ask another student in each group to construct a set of blocks with the same color but more sides than your block. Ask a third student to select a set of blocks with the same number of sides but a different color than your block. Repeat the activity using other shapes and colors as time permits.

Remove the small blocks from their containers and return the large blocks to their proper locations. Distribute Activity Sheet 209. Working with groups of three, ask one group to construct a set by selecting all the blocks with four sides from their set of ATTRIBUTE BLOCKS. Next, ask the other group to construct a second block set by removing all the red blocks from the first group's set. Encourage the students to describe the common attributes of the set. Allow time for the students to place the blocks in the box, trace them, and color the pictures before distributing Activity Sheet 210. Repeat the procedure for a set of thin blue shapes. Continue emphasizing the common attributes of the final set.

Forming a Group—Shape and Color (Activity 211–212)

Objectives:
Using ATTRIBUTE BLOCKS:
1. classify blocks according to a single attribute
2. construct a set of blocks that satisfies two attributes

Materials:
For each group of six students • One set of ATTRIBUTE BLOCKS

For each student   • Activity Sheets 211–212
                                             • Crayons

Teacher Instructions:
This lesson using ATTRIBUTE BLOCKS continues the task of constructing a set according to two common attributes. The initial activity introduces the word "not" to identify blocks with attributes opposite to those of a given block. Encourage the students to verbalize the attributes of the sets by incorporating the word "not" into their description. For example, stress that a set containing both yellow and blue blocks can be described by the attribute "not red."

Classroom Activity:
After separating the ATTRIBUTE BLOCKS into large and small shapes, return the small blocks to their containers and ask each group of six students to sort the large blocks by thickness to provide one group of three students with the fifteen thick blocks and the other with the fifteen thin blocks. Hold up a **large red hexagon-shape** and ask one student in each group of three to locate all the blocks that have the *same* number of sides as your block. Ask a second student in each group to remove all the blocks with the same color as your block from the constructed set and return them to the original pile. Ask the students to compare the set of remaining blocks to the block you are holding. Discuss with the students that all the blocks in their sets have the same shape, but a different color than your block. Repeat the activity using blocks of other shapes and colors as time permits.

Remove the small blocks from their containers, return the large blocks to their proper locations, and distribute Activity Sheets 211 and 212. Working with groups of three, ask one group to construct a set by selecting all the blocks with round shapes from their set of ATTRIBUTE BLOCKS. Then ask the other group to remove all the blue blocks from this constructed set. Encourage the students to use the word "not" when describing the attributes of the remaining set. Have the groups return all the small blocks to the pile, then reverse the groups' roles and repeat the procedure, asking one group to construct a set of all the thin shapes and the other group to remove the round blocks from that set. Continue to emphasize use of "not" to describe the attribute of the remaining set. Alternate the tasks between the two groups and allow time for each student to place the correct blocks in the boxes on the sheets, trace the blocks, and color the pictures.

Forming a Group—Shape (Activity 213–214)

Objectives:
Using PATTERN BLOCKS:
1. classify blocks according to a single attribute
2. construct a set that satisfies one of two attributes

Materials:
For each group of six students • One set of PATTERN BLOCKS

For each student   • Activity Sheets 213–214
                                    • Crayons

Teacher Instructions:
This activity uses PATTERN BLOCKS rather than ATTRIBUTE BLOCKS to continue the task of constructing a set of shapes with one or more attributes in common. Since the activity again uses "number of sides" as an attribute, different shapes and colors of blocks will be included in the same set. The word "or" used as a logical connective is also introduced to describe and construct sets containing blocks that satisfy *either* of two attributes defined in a statement. Students should be encouraged to verbalize the attributes of the sets and to indicate which of the properties are satisfied. (For example, "It is a square, but not a triangle.")

Classroom Activity:
Ask each student to select three different blocks from the PATTERN BLOCK set. Hold up a **square** (orange) and ask whether any students have selected a square. Discuss the attributes of the square, focusing on the fact that it has four sides. Ask the students whether any have other shapes with four sides. After they combine all the blocks with four sides into a set, encourage the students to verbalize the attributes of that set. Return the students' blocks to the original set, then ask the students to select three other blocks with different shapes. Hold up a **trapezoid** (red) and ask whether any students have selected that block. Combine the trapezoids to form a set, then hold up a **hexagon** (yellow) and ask whether any students have selected that block. Place the hexagons with the trapezoids and discuss the attributes of the combined set with the students. Encourage them to use the word "or" to define the set. (Each block in the set is *either* a trapezoid *or* a hexagon….is *either* yellow *or* red, etc.)

Distribute Activity Sheet 213 and ask the students to locate blocks to cover the pictured shapes. Discuss the attribute of the blocks in the set, focusing on the number of sides on the various blocks. Allow time for the students to move all the blocks with four sides to the box at the bottom of the sheet, trace the blocks and color the pictures. Distribute Activity Sheet 214 and again ask the students to cover the pictured shapes. As you point to a rhombus, ask the students if the block is a square or a triangle (no). Continue questioning the students on specific blocks, having them move the appropriate blocks into the box.

107

Groups with Common Elements (Activity 215–216)

Objectives:
Using PATTERN BLOCKS:
1. match blocks with pictures of shapes
2. identify common shapes in different sets

Materials:
For each group of six students • One set of PATTERN BLOCKS

For each student   • Activity Sheets 215–216
                                              • Crayons

Teacher Instructions:
This lesson uses PATTERN BLOCKS to introduce the skill of finding elements (blocks) common to two sets. The concept underlying these activities involves identification of the *intersection* of two sets. Since the Activity Sheets include sets that have more than one shape in common, discuss with the students the need to continue their search after they locate the first set of matching blocks. In addition, matching blocks have been placed in different positions and the students should be reminded that turning and/or flipping a block does not change its shape.

Classroom Activity:
Ask each student to remove one or two handsful of blocks from their PATTERN BLOCKS to form a set. Hold up a **tan rhombus** and ask the students if they can find the same shape in their sets. Determine which students have a matching block and stress that the diamond is a common block in those sets. Hold up a **blue rhombus** and repeat the process. Again emphasize the idea of comparing sets to determine which sets have a blue rhombus as a common shape. Discuss the task of finding other blocks that are the same shape in the sets. Next, with the students working in pairs, have one of each pair select a block from the set and the other student search the second set for the same block. Repeat the activity as time permits.

Allow the students to continue to work in pairs and distribute Activity Sheet 215. Each student should select the blocks needed to cover the shapes pictured in one set in Exercise **A**. After they complete the task, encourage the students to describe the set they have created. Then ask them to compare the two sets to decide which block is the same in both sets. Allow time for the students to color the matching shapes, then repeat the process with Exercise **B**. Encourage the students to compare all the blocks in the two sets, since there may be more than one pair of matching shapes. After they complete the sheet, distribute Activity Sheet 216 and permit students to continue working in pairs, constructing the two sets and locating the elements that are the same in both sets. Again, stress the need to compare each different block in the first set to each block in the second.

Groups with Common Elements (Activity 217–218)

Objectives:
Using INTERLOCKING CUBES:
1. construct figures to match pictures
2. identify common figures in different sets

Materials:
For each group of six students • One set of INTERLOCKING CUBES

For each student   • Activity Sheets 217–218
                          • Crayons

Teacher Instructions:
This lesson continues to develop the ability of finding elements (figures) common to two sets. The basic concept presented revolves around the task of identifying the intersection of two sets. The matching process requires that students locate figures that are in both set A and set B. Since the Activity Sheets include sets with more than one figure in common, discuss with the students the need to continue searching after they locate the first set of matching figures. Once again, matching figures have been placed in different positions and the students should be reminded that turning and/or flipping a figure does not alter its shape.

Classroom Activity:
Ask each student to form a set of twenty cubes with the same color and to construct the following figures: two T-shapes of four cubes each, two L-shapes of four cubes each, and two lengths two with the remaining cubes. With the students working in pairs, first ask each pair to combine their two sets of figures, then to separate the collected sets randomly to form two new sets. Ask one student to select a figure from one set and the other to search the other set for a matching figure. Reverse the students' roles and repeat the process to locate other matching figures. Stress that the matched figures are common to *both* sets.

Distribute Activity Sheet 217 and allow the students to continue working in pairs. Ask one student in each pair to select the set of cubes necessary to cover the white figures pictured in both boxes while the other selects a different set of cubes to cover the shaded figures. After they complete the selection, construct the figures, and cover the pictures on one student's sheet, encourage the students to compare the sets of figures. (Each set has three different shapes and two different colors.) Next, ask the students to compare the two sets and determine which figures are the same in both sets. Encourage students to compare all the figures, since more than one pair of matching shapes is possible, and to explain why some figures are not common to the two sets (e.g., same shape, but different color, etc.). After students color the pictures, distribute Activity Sheet 218 and permit students to continue to work in pairs on the remaining exercises to select the cubes, construct the figures, and locate the matching elements in both sets. Again, stress the need to compare each different figure in the first set to those in the second.

109

Groups with Common Elements (Activity 219–220)

Objectives:

Using ATTRIBUTE BLOCKS:
1. match blocks with pictures of shapes
2. identify common shapes in different sets

Materials:

For each group of six students • One set of ATTRIBUTE BLOCKS

For each student   • Activity Sheets 219–220
                                              • Crayons

Teacher Instructions:

This lesson uses ATTRIBUTE BLOCKS to conclude the series of activities on finding elements common to two sets. The basic concept presented in these activities revolves around the task of identifying the intersection of two sets. The matching process requires the location of shapes that are in *both set A and set B*. Since the Activity Sheets again include sets with more than one shape in common, discuss with the students the need to continue their search after they locate the first pair of matching shapes. In addition, since both thick and thin blocks are needed to cover the pictured shapes, stress that the attribute of thickness should be ignored.

Classroom Activity:

Separate the ATTRIBUTE BLOCKS into large and small shapes and assign a size to each group of three students. Ask each group to separate the blocks by color, creating three sets. Ask the students in each group to take turns selecting blocks from the three sets until all the blocks are chosen and each student has created a new set containing all shapes and colors. (Each student should have ten blocks.) Ask one student in each group to select a block from his/her set and ask the other students whether they have a block with the same shape and color in their sets. Stress that each set of large or small blocks has only one other block that is both the same shape and color. Encourage the students to verbalize comparative attributes, i.e., whether they have blocks that are the same color but a different shape, or blocks that are the same shape but a different color. Repeat the process, rotating the tasks among students and locating other matching shapes.

Separate the blocks by size and return the large blocks to their containers. Distribute Activity Sheets 219 and 220, and allow the students to continue working in groups of three to cover the shapes pictured in the two boxes on one student's sheet.Then ask each group to compare the two sets and decide which blocks are the same in both sets. Encourage the students to compare all the blocks, since more than one pair of matching shapes is possible, and to explain why some blocks are not common to the two sets. (e.g., They have the same shape, but a different color.) Allow time for the students to complete each individual's Activity Sheets, rotating the tasks by having the groups alternate between sheets.

Defining a Group (Activity 221–222)

Objectives:
Using ATTRIBUTE BLOCKS:
1. classify blocks according to a single attribute
2. determine the blocks that belong to a set

Materials:

For each group of six students • One set of ATTRIBUTE BLOCKS

For each student • Activity Sheets 221–222
• Crayons

Teacher Instructions:
This lesson uses ATTRIBUTE BLOCKS to further the task of defining a set of shapes according to a common attribute. Since the groups of shapes pictured on the Activity Sheets are smaller than the actual blocks, students can no longer construct the sets by placing the blocks directly over the pictures. Students who are unable to define the attributes of the groups from the pictures may be allowed to reconstruct the sets, or, as an intermediate process, a visual cue can be provided by coloring the pictures of the shapes in each group.

Classroom Activity:
After separating the ATTRIBUTE BLOCKS into large and small shapes, return the large blocks to their containers. Ask each group of six students to sort the blocks by thickness and assign each set to a group of three students. Ask the students with the thin blocks to sort their set by color, providing each student with a set of blocks. Ask the students with the thick blocks to sort their set by shape, providing each student with one of the following sets: **hexagon-shapes**, **square-shapes**, or **circle-shapes**. Discuss the properties of the sets that they have selected with the students (same color, all shapes or same shape, all colors). Hold up a **red hexagon-shape** and help the students determine the sets in which the block could be placed (the red shapes or the hexagon-shapes). Stress that the attribute of thickness should be ignored. Repeat the task with a **circle-shape** and a **square-shape** of different colors.

Distribute Activity Sheet 221, then discuss the attributes of the two sets of shapes pictured at the top of the sheet. Encourage the students to verbalize the property common to all the shapes in the first set (all red) and to compare the two sets to determine why the shapes in the bottom set do not belong in the top set (none are red). Ask each group of three students to select the correct blocks to cover the pictures at the bottom of the sheet; then work with the students to determine whether or not each block belongs to the group defined by the two sets at the top of the sheet. Rotate the task among the students in each group and allow time for them to complete the coloring activity. Distribute Activity Sheet 222 and repeat the process, first identifying the attributes of the group of blocks defined by the two sets at the top of the page, then deciding which blocks on the bottom of the sheet belong to the group.

Common Properties (Activity 223–224)

Objectives:

Using ATTRIBUTE BLOCKS:
  1. classify blocks according to two attributes
  2. construct an array having two attributes

Materials:

For each group of six students • One set of ATTRIBUTE BLOCKS

For each student   • Activity Sheets 223–224
                                            • Crayons

Teacher Instructions:

This lesson uses ATTRIBUTE BLOCKS to introduce the task of forming an array based on two attributes. Each block in the array must simultaneously conform to the row attribute (shape) and to the column attribute (color). Tasks on the Activity Sheets may be treated as a two part activity: first locating all the blocks with the same shape as the row picture; then selecting the block from that set with the same color as the column picture. Reference can also be made to the illustration at the top of the first page, which defines the attributes used in the other three exercises.

Classroom Activity:

After separating the ATTRIBUTE BLOCKS into large and small shapes, ask each group of six students to sort the blocks by thickness, creating a total of four sets, and to select one set for each pair of students. Ask one student from each pair to locate all the **hexagon-shapes** and place them in a row, beginning with the red one. Discuss the properties of the blocks in the row with the students. Then ask the other student in each pair to remove all the remaining **red shapes** from the set. That student should then make a column of the red shapes beneath the red hexagon-shape. Ask the first student to build a second row using the shapes that match the red block beneath the red hexagon-shape. Stress that the color of each block placed beneath a hexagon-shape must match the color of that hexagon-shape. Build a second column based on color and continue the process until all the blocks have been placed in the array. (Each row has the same shapes and each column has the same color.)

Distribute Activity Sheets 223 and 224 and work with the students to construct the array of blocks pictured at the top of Sheet 223. Encourage the students to verbalize the common property of the shapes that form each row (same shape) and those in each column (same color). Allow the students to color the pictures; then continue the task with different pairs of students working on different exercises on the two sheets. Students should cover the pictures of the shapes and decide which block is needed to complete the array. Work with individual pairs, encouraging them to identify the attribute common to each row (shape) and column (color) in the array.

Common Properties (Activity 225–226)

Objectives:
Using ATTRIBUTE BLOCKS:
1. classify blocks according to two attributes
2. construct an array having two attributes

Materials:

For each group of six students • One set of ATTRIBUTE BLOCKS

For each student   • Activity Sheets 225–226
                                            • Crayons

Teacher Instructions:
This lesson uses ATTRIBUTE BLOCKS to continue the task of forming arrays based on two attributes. Each block in the array must simultaneously conform to the row attribute (shape) and the column attribute (color). The Activity Sheets can again be treated as a two-part activity, with students first locating all the blocks that are the same shape as the row picture, and then selecting the block from that set that is the same color as the column picture. Since some exercises require students to locate two missing blocks in the array, the complexity level on the Activity Sheets has also been increased.

Classroom Activity:
Separate the ATTRIBUTE BLOCKS into large and small shapes, then ask each group of six students to sort the blocks by thickness to create a total of four sets, and have each pair choose a set. Ask one student in each pair to locate all the blue blocks and place them in a column beginning with the **blue rectangle-shape**. Discuss the properties of the blocks in the column with the students. Next, ask the other student in each pair to remove all the **rectangle-shapes** from the remaining set. That student should then make a row of shapes beginning with the blue rectangle-shape in the original column. Hold up a **yellow square-shape** and ask the students to select a block with the same color and shape from their sets. Discuss with the students where the block should be placed in the array. (Responses will differ from pair to pair, depending on the block arrangements.) Repeat the task, alternating construction of rows and columns, and use the remaining blocks to complete the array.

Distribute Activity Sheets 225 and 226 and work with the students to construct the array of blocks pictured at the top of Sheet 225. Encourage the students to verbalize the common property of the shapes in each row (same shape) and the common attribute of the shapes in each column (same color). Allow pairs of students to work on different exercises on the two sheets, covering the pictured shapes, deciding which block or blocks are needed to complete the array, and coloring the pictures. Work with individual pairs, encouraging them to identify the attribute common to each row (shape) and column (color) in each array.

114

ANALOGIES

Shape and Color (Activity 227–228)

Objectives:

Using ATTRIBUTE BLOCKS:
1. match blocks with pictures of shapes
2. define a relationship between pairs of shapes
3. complete an analogy involving two attributes

Materials:

For each group of three students • One set of ATTRIBUTE BLOCKS

For each student
- Activity Sheets 227–228
- Crayons

Teacher Instructions:

Using ATTRIBUTE BLOCKS, this lesson begins developing the concept of an analogy by comparing the attributes of shape and color. This task differs from earlier work with sequences, since the selection of the fourth block in each row is based upon the relationship between blocks one and two, not the relationship between blocks two and three. Encourage the students to focus on the relationship of attributes between the first two blocks, then to select a block that relates to the third block in the same manner. Because a number of blocks with the same color and same shape are required for some constructions, each group of three, rather than six, students should have access to one complete set of blocks.

Classroom Activity:

After separating the ATTRIBUTE BLOCKS into large and small shapes, return the large blocks to their containers. Divide the class into groups of three, with each group having access to one set of small blocks. Hold up a **red** and a **yellow square-shape**, and ask each group to locate the same blocks in their set, ignoring thickness. Encourage the students to compare the attributes of the two blocks (same shape and size, different colors). Next, hold up a **red circle-shape** and discuss with the students which block should be selected to show the same relationship as the one they described between the square shapes (yellow circle-shape). Place the four blocks in a row, beginning with the red, then yellow, square-shapes, and encourage the students to verbalize the relationships between the first and second blocks and between the third and fourth blocks in the row. Repeat the activity, holding up two **blue hexagon-shapes** followed by a **red rectangle-shape**. After discussing the relationship, ask the students to find a fourth block to complete the analogy.

Distribute Activity Sheets 227 and 228 and continue working with groups of three. Help the students locate the blocks to cover the shapes pictured at the top of sheet 227. Then ask them to choose blocks to cover the remaining shapes on the sheet. Discuss with the students the relationship between the first two blocks in Row **A**. Work with them to decide which block from the top of the sheet should be placed in the dotted box (blue square-shape). Continue to work on the remaining exercises, allowing time for the students to trace the blocks and color the pictures.

Shape and Color (Activity 229–230)

Objectives:
> Using ATTRIBUTE BLOCKS:
> 1. match blocks with pictures of shapes
> 2. define a relationship between pairs of shapes
> 3. complete an analogy involving two attributes

Materials:
> For each group of three students   • One set of ATTRIBUTE BLOCKS
>
> For each student   • Activity Sheets 229–230
>   • Crayons

Teacher Instructions:
> This lesson continues to develop the concept of an analogy using ATTRIBUTE BLOCKS. The tasks again use the attributes of shape and color to define a relationship between the first two blocks in each row. Continue encouraging students to focus on the comparative attributes of the first two blocks, then selecting a block that relates to the third block in the same manner. Stress that the selection of the fourth block in each row is based upon the relationship between the first and second blocks, not upon the relationship between the second and third blocks. Because a number of blocks with the same color and same shape are required to complete the activities, each group of three students should have access to one set of blocks.

Classroom Activity:
> After separating the ATTRIBUTE BLOCKS into large and small shapes, return the large blocks to their containers. Divide the class into groups of three, with each group having access to one set of small blocks. Hold up two different-colored **circle-shapes**, and ask two students in each group to choose the matching blocks (ignoring thickness) from their sets (a total of four blocks) and place them in two rows. Encourage the students to verbalize the comparative attributes of the two blocks in each row (same shape, different colors). Next, ask the third student in each group to select two blocks that are not circle-shapes, but that have the same comparative attributes. (There are four possible choices.) Work with the groups to create an analogy using one pair of circle-shapes and the two blocks selected by the third student. Repeat the task, creating a second analogy using the second pair of circle-shapes and a different pair of blocks from the set. Encourage students to verbalize the relationships between the first and second blocks and between the third and fourth blocks in each row.
>
> Distribute Activity Sheets 229 and 230 and continue working with groups of three. Allow time for the students to cover the pictures on sheet 229 of one student in each group. Encourage them to verbalize the relationship between the first two blocks in Row **A**, emphasizing the comparative attributes of the pair. Then work with the students to determine which block should be placed in the dotted box (red hexagon-shape). Assist students with the remaining exercises on the two sheets, rotating the tasks and allowing time to trace the blocks and color the pictures.

Shape and Size (Activity 231–232)

Objectives:
Using ATTRIBUTE BLOCKS:
1. match blocks with pictures of shapes
2. define a relationship between pairs of shapes
3. complete an analogy involving two attributes

Materials:
For each group of six students • One set of ATTRIBUTE BLOCKS

For each student   • Activity Sheets 231–232
                                                    • Crayons

Teacher Instructions:
This lesson further develops the concept of analogy using ATTRIBUTE BLOCKS, by introducing the attributes of shape and size to define a relationship. Continue encouraging students to focus their attention on the comparative attributes of the first two blocks, then to select a block that relates to the third block in the same manner. Stress again that the selection of the fourth block for each row is based upon the relationship between the first and second blocks, not upon the relationship between the second and third blocks.

Classroom Activity:
After separating the ATTRIBUTE BLOCKS into thick and thin shapes, ask the students to further sort the blocks by color to create one set of six blocks for each student. Hold up a **large red triangle-shape** and a **large red square-shape**, asking which students have the same blocks in their sets. After those two students have selected the matching blocks and placed them in a row, encourage students to verbalize the comparative attributes of the two blocks. (They have the same color and size, but different shapes.) Help the students locate two **small** blocks showing the same relationship and create an analogy by adding these blocks to the row. Encourage students to verbalize the relationships between the first and second blocks and the third and fourth blocks in the row. Repeat the task using other pairs of blocks and the attributes of shape and size. Color should remain constant within each row.

Regroup the set of blocks by thickness to provide each group of three students with a complete set of thick or thin blocks. After distributing Activity Sheet 231, allow time for each group to locate blocks to cover the pictures on one student's sheet. Discuss the relationship between the first two blocks in Row **A** with the students, emphasizing the comparative attributes of that pair. (They have the same size and color, but different shapes.) Then work with the students to decide which block has the same relationship to the third block and should be placed in the dotted box (small yellow square-shape). Assist students with the remaining exercises, and continue the task on Activity Sheet 232, allowing time for students to trace the blocks and color the pictures.

Shape, Color, and Size (Activity 233–234)

Objectives:
>   Using ATTRIBUTE BLOCKS:
>   1. match blocks with pictures of shapes
>   2. define a relationship between pairs of shapes
>   3. complete an analogy involving three attributes

Materials:
>   For each group of six students • One set of ATTRIBUTE BLOCKS
>
>   For each student   • Activity Sheets 233–234
>   • Crayons

Teacher Instructions:
>   This lesson is the last in a series of activities exploring the concept of analogy using ATTRIBUTE BLOCKS. These tasks include using the attributes of shape, color, and size to define a relationship between the first two blocks in each row. The first and second blocks in each analogy have one attribute in common (shape, color, or size), and that attribute remains constant for the third and fourth blocks in that analogy. Continue encouraging students to focus on comparing the attributes of the first two blocks, then selecting a fourth block that relates to the third one in the same manner.

Classroom Activity:
>   After separating the ATTRIBUTE BLOCKS into thick and thin shapes, assign one set (thick or thin) to each group of three students. Hold up a **large red circle-shape** and a **small blue circle-shape**, and ask the students to select the same blocks from their sets and place them in a row. Encourage students to compare the attributes of the two blocks (different color and size, same shape). Then hold up a **large red hexagon-shape**, asking the groups to locate that block and add it to their rows. Work with the students to decide which block should be added to complete the analogy (small blue hexagon-shape). Continue to encourage students to verbalize the relationships between the first and second blocks and the third and fourth blocks. Repeat the task, using the attributes of shape, color, and size with other pairs of blocks and keeping one of the three attributes constant in each analogy.
>
>   Distribute Activity Sheet 233 and allow time for each group of three to locate the blocks and cover the pictures in Row **A** on one student's sheet. Discuss the relationship between the first two blocks in the row with the students, emphasizing the comparative attributes of that pair. Use these same attributes with the third block to determine which block should be placed in the dotted box (large yellow hexagon-shape). Distribute Activity Sheet 234 and have students work individually on different exercises to complete the activity. Encourage students to use the attributes of shape, color, and size to explain the properties of each analogy.

Shape and Position (Activity 235–236)

Objectives:
Using PATTERN BLOCKS:
1. match blocks with pictures of shapes
2. define a relationship between pairs of shapes
3. complete an analogy involving two attributes

Materials:

For each group of six students • One set of PATTERN BLOCKS

For each student　　　　　　　• Activity Sheets 235–236
　　　　　　　　　　　　　　　• Crayons

Teacher Instructions:
This lesson uses PATTERN BLOCKS to continue developing the ability to analyze and create analogies. Since the initial activities require students to create analogies based upon the position of the blocks, it may be necessary to remind them that blocks may be turned and/or flipped without changing their shape. Because verbally describing placement is difficult, check each row of blocks as the lesson progresses to insure that students have created the correct analogy. Several exercises include more than one possible correct response, depending upon whether students see the blocks as having been turned or flipped.

Classroom Activity:
Ask students to select two **trapezoids** (red) and two **hexagons** (yellow) from their set of PATTERN BLOCKS. Have them place the trapezoids in a row with the long sides on the bottom, then turn the second one to the right (clockwise) until the long side is pointing upward (one-fourth of a complete rotation). After discussing the relationship between the two trapezoids, add one hexagon to the row and work with the students to decide the position the other hexagon must have to complete the analogy. Repeat the activity using **squares** (orange) and **rhombuses** (tan). Turn the second square 45 degrees (one-eighth of a complete rotation), and stress that the rhombus in the fourth position should also be turned one-eighth of a complete rotation. There may be alternative answers, since students will have no way of identifying the direction of the rotation.

After distributing Activity Sheet 235, allow time for the students to select blocks and cover the pictures on the sheet. Discuss the relationship between the first and second blocks in Row **A** (same shape, turned clockwise), and work with the students to decide which block from the top of the sheet should be placed in the dotted box (trapezoid). Next, ask them to describe the position in which the trapezoid must be placed to complete the analogy. Work with the students to complete the remaining exercises on the sheet, and allow time for the tracing and coloring activity. Distribute Activity Sheet 236 and permit students to continue independently with the tasks. Work with individual students, encouraging them to verbalize the comparative properties of each analogy. Emphasize the turning and/or flipping of the blocks as a key aspect of each analogy.

Shape and Position (Activity 237–238)

Objectives:
>Using PATTERN BLOCKS:
>1. match blocks with pictures of shapes and figures
>2. define a relationship between pairs of shapes of figures
>3. complete an analogy involving two attributes

Materials:
>For each group of six students • One set of PATTERN BLOCKS
>
>For each student   • Activity Sheets 237–238
>   • Crayons

Teacher Instructions:
>This activity continues to use PATTERN BLOCKS for developing the ability to analyze and create analogies. The task's complexity is increased, since some exercises include analogies based upon the attributes of figures formed by combining shapes. Initial activities require the students to create analogies based upon the position of the blocks. Since verbally describing placement is difficult, check each row of blocks as the lesson progresses to insure that the students have created the correct analogy. Several exercises may have more than one possible correct response, depending upon whether students see the blocks as having been turned or flipped.

Classroom Activity:
>Ask each student to select two **blue rhombuses** and two **tan rhombuses** from their set of PATTERN BLOCKS, then to create two different figures by placing one blue rhombus above one tan rhombus and the other blue rhombus beneath the second tan one. (The shapes should be stacked to form two "towers.") Have the students place the two figures in a row, then discuss the relationship between the two figures in terms of the positions of the blocks. Next, ask each student to select two **green triangles** and two additional **blue rhombuses** from the set. Using these blocks, work with the students to complete an analogy with the rhombuses in the same relative positions. Repeat the activity, using other block combinations as time permits.
>
>Distribute Activity Sheet 237 and allow students time to select the blocks and cover the pictured shapes. Discuss the relationship between the first two blocks in Row **A** (same shape, different position), and work with the students to determine which block to place in the dotted box (hexagon). Ask the students to describe the position in which the hexagon must be placed to complete the analogy. Allow time for the students to trace the blocks and color the pictures, then work with them to complete the remaining exercises on the sheet. Distribute Activity Sheet 238 and ask the students to construct the figures for the first three pictures in Row **A**. Encourage them to verbalize the relationship between the first two figures of the analogy, focusing their attention on the role of turning and/or flipping the figures as a key aspect of the analogy. Allow students to complete the sheet individually.

Shape (Activity 239–240)

Objectives:
Using PATTERN BLOCKS:
1. construct figures to match pictures
2. define a relationship between pairs of figures
3. complete an analogy involving a single attribute

Materials:
For each group of six students • One set of PATTERN BLOCKS

For each student   • Activity Sheets 239–240
                               • Crayons

Teacher Instructions:
This is the last lesson in the series employing PATTERN BLOCKS to explore the properties of analogies. Both the initial activities and the Activity Sheets include analogies based upon the attributes of figures formed by combining shapes. Since the placement of figures in the initial task is difficult to verbalize, check each row as the lesson progresses to insure that the students have created the appropriate analogy. Several exercises may have more than one possible correct response, depending upon whether students see the figures as having been turned or flipped.

Classroom Activity:
Divide each group into pairs, and ask one of each pair to select two **hexagons** (yellow) and the other to select two **trapezoids** (red) and two **rhombuses** (blue) from the PATTERN BLOCK set. Help them create two figures by placing one rhombus above one hexagon and one trapezoid beneath the second hexagon (shapes should be stacked to form a "tower"). Have the students place the two figures in a row, and encourage them to discuss the relationship between the figures in terms of the locations of the hexagons. Then ask the first student to select two **squares** (orange) from the set of blocks. Work with the student to complete the analogy by combining the squares and remaining blocks (one trapezoid and one rhombus) so that the squares are in the same relative positions as the hexagons. Repeat the activity using other blocks and alternating the roles between the students.

After distributing Activity Sheet 239, allow students time to construct and cover the figures pictured in Row **A**. Discuss the relationship between the first two figures in the row, emphasizing the position of the square in relation to the other blocks. Then work with the students to decide which blocks they will need to construct the figure for the dotted box (a hexagon above a trapezoid). Allow time for the tracing and coloring activity; then work with the students to complete the remaining exercise on the sheet. Distribute Activity Sheet 240 and ask the students to construct and cover the first three figures of the analogy in Row **A**. Again, encourage students to verbalize the relationship between the first two figures of the analogy, focusing their attention on the presence of the same shape in each one.

Patterns (Activity 241–242)

Objectives:
Using INTERLOCKING CUBES:
1. construct figures to match pictures
2. define a relationship between pairs of figures
3. complete an analogy involving two attributes

Materials:

For each group of six students • One set of INTERLOCKING CUBES

For each student   • Activity Sheets 241–242
                                • Crayons

Teacher Instructions:
This lesson begins a series using the attributes of color pattern, position, and number of cubes (shape) in INTERLOCKING CUBE figures to analyze and construct analogies. Continue to encourage the students to view each row of figures as an analogy, rather than a sequence, by stressing the relationship between the first two figures as the basis for determining which figure to select for the fourth item in each row. Emphasize that the relationship between the third and fourth figures in an analogy must satisfy the same conditions as the relationship between the first and second figures in that row.

Classroom Activity:
Ask each student to select two ten-cube sets from their set of INTERLOCKING CUBES, with each set a different color. Ask each student to construct **two lengths of three cubes** and **one length of two cubes** from each color set, leaving two single cubes of each color. Students should then select one length of three and a single cube of the same color and place them in a row with the single cube first. Ask the students to place a single cube of a different color next in the row. Help the students compare the first two figures in their row, encouraging them to verbalize the relationship. (The figures are the same color, but the second has two cubes more than the first.) Then work with the students to decide which of their constructed figures should be added to the row to complete the analogy. Repeat the activity using other combinations of the constructed figures.

Distribute Activity Sheet 241 and allow time for each student to construct and cover the figures pictured at the top of the sheet. Ask the students to locate the figures to cover the three pictures in Row **A**. Encourage them to explain the relationship between the first two figures in the row. (They have the same color and position, but the second figure has one more cube.) Let students decide which figure from the top of the sheet should be selected to complete the analogy, again asking them to state the relationship. Allow time for them to trace the figures and color the pictures; then repeat the process for Rows **B** and **C**. Distribute Activity Sheet 242 and work with the students to construct the required figures and complete each analogy. After students cover the pictures in each row, encourage them to describe the relationships between the figures using the attributes of color pattern, position, and number of cubes.

122

Shape and Pattern (Activity 243–244)

Objectives:
Using INTERLOCKING CUBES:
1. construct figures to match pictures
2. define a relationship between pairs of figures
3. complete an analogy based on two attributes

Materials:
For each group of six students • One set of INTERLOCKING CUBES

For each student   • Activity Sheets 243–244
                                    • Crayons

Teacher Instructions:
This lesson is second in the series using INTERLOCKING CUBE figures to analyze and construct analogies based on the attributes of color pattern and number of cubes. Continue to encourage the students to view each row of figures as an analogy rather than a sequence, stressing that a complete analogy requires that the relationship between the third and fourth figures in each row must satisfy the same conditions as the relationship between the first and second figures.

Classroom Activity:
Ask each student to select two ten-cube sets of INTERLOCKING CUBES, with each set a different color. When they have chosen their sets, ask them to construct **four lengths of three cubes** and **two lengths of two cubes** using the following alternating color patterns: XOX; XOX; OXO; OXO; OX; and XO. Two single cubes should be left in each set. Students should then select one length of three and a single cube with the same color as two of the cubes in the length and place them in a row, single cube first (X, XOX, for example). Then ask the students to add a single cube a different color than the other single cube to their row. Encourage the students to compare the first two figures in the row and verbalize the relationship between them. (The single cube is the same color as two cubes in the length, and the second figure has two cubes more than the first.) Help the students determine which constructed figure can be added to the row to complete the analogy. Repeat the activity using other combinations of the constructed figures.

Distribute Activity Sheet 243, allowing time for students to select the cubes and construct the figures pictured in Row **A**. After they cover the pictures, encourage them to explain the relationship between the first two figures in the row. (One cube has been added to the second figure to continue the alternating-color pattern.) Help the students decide how to construct a figure to complete the analogy. Allow time for coloring, then repeat the process for Rows **B** and **C**. Distribute Activity Sheet 244 and work with the students to construct the necessary figures and complete each analogy. After they cover the figures pictured in each row, encourage the students to describe the relationships between the figures using the attributes of color pattern and number of cubes.

Shape and Pattern (Activity 245–246)

Objectives:
Using INTERLOCKING CUBES:
1. construct figures to match pictures
2. define a relationship between pairs of figures
3. complete an analogy involving two attributes

Materials:
For each group of six students • One set of INTERLOCKING CUBES

For each student   • Activity Sheets 245–246
                                              • Crayons

Teacher Instructions:
This lesson uses the attributes of shape, color pattern, and number of cubes to conclude the series using INTERLOCKING CUBE figures to analyze and construct analogies. Continue encouraging the students to view each row of figures as an analogy rather than a sequence, stressing that the relationship between the first two figures in each row is the basis for determining what should be constructed for the fourth figure. Emphasize that the relationship between the third and fourth figures must satisfy the same conditions as the relationship between the first and second figures.

Classroom Activity:
Ask each student to select two ten-cube sets of INTERLOCKING CUBES, with each set a different color. Ask the students to construct **one two-by-two cube square, one length of two cubes,** and **one three-cube L-shape** with each color, leaving one cube in each color set. Students should select an L-shape and a square of the same color and place them in a row, the L-shape first. Next, ask the students to choose an L-shape of a different color to add to the row. Encourage them to compare the first two figures in their row and verbalize the relationship between them. (They are the same color, but the second figure has one cube more than the first.) Then work with the students to determine which construction should be added to the row to complete the analogy. Repeat the activity as time permits, using the other constructed figures.

Distribute Activity Sheet 245 and allow time for each student to select cubes to construct and cover the figures pictured in Row **A**. Encourage the students to explain the relationship between the first two figures in the row. (They are the same color, but one cube has been added to the second figure to make an upside-down L-shape.) After they describe figure three, help them decide how to construct a figure to complete the analogy. Allow time for coloring, then repeat the process for Rows **B** and **C**. Distribute Activity Sheet 246 and work with the students to construct the necessary figures and complete each analogy. After they cover the figures pictured in each row, encourage the students to describe the relationships between figures using the attributes of shape, color pattern, and number of cubes.